The Lord Jesus Christ could ha~
standing on the ground (Titus
could have returned before the
did not. He could return today at any moment. But what if He tarries
and the US is still here to go through the Tribulation after the Rapture?
It takes an erudite historian, political scientist, and author to project what
the world would look like if America were still a driving force during the
time of the antichrist. This is exactly what Jeremy Stevens projects for
you in his analysis of contemporary world history with the US as a driving and providential force, in *So...What Happens Next? Exploring Biblical
Prophecies to Make Sense of Today's Chaos.*

J.O. HOSLER, THD, SENIOR PASTOR
NAPIER PARKVIEW BAPTIST CHURCH, BENTON HARBOR, MI

This is a timely, well-researched, thought-provoking book that takes us
on a tour of biblical prophecy. You'll find answers and encourage-
ment for end times in these pages!

LARRY STARKEY, PASTOR
GRACE FELLOWSHIP, WEST PALM BEACH, FL

So What Happens Next?

JEREMY STEVENS

So What
Happens NEXT?

EXPLORING BIBLICAL PROPHECIES TO MAKE
SENSE OF TODAY'S CHAOS

Published by
Deep River Books
Sisters, Oregon
www.deepriverbooks.com

ISBN–13: 9781937756468
ISBN–10: 1937756467

Library of Congress: 2012948742

Printed in the USA

Cover design by David Litwin, Pure Fusion Media

DEDICATION

To my wonderful wife, family, and friends, and to the most important
and influential Bible teachers I had—my parents.

CONTENTS

INTRODUCTION

Mankind has always been obsessed with the future. Charlatans such as tarot seers and psychics charge hefty fees to give customers vague predictions. "You will meet the love of your life soon," or, "One day you will run into a lot of money." Psychics usually shy away from negative predictions, such as, "You will have a massive heart-attack on your way to work," or "The TV hit *Jersey Shore* is signing on for twenty more years."

Ancient civilizations were just as preoccupied. Great kings and generals, from Alexander the Great to Caesar Augustus, would trek to the mountainous city of Delphi in Greece where the Oracle would foretell their futures. Average folk would pay heavy fees to seers and prophets to have their futures told as well.

In modern times, our particular obsession with the future regards the end of the world, a rather morbid fascination I find myself strangely drawn to as well. The latest rave was the Mayan prediction of 2012. It fit so timely with the environmental doom of global warming, or is it climate change now? Did the Mayans really predict the end of the world? Or did they just get lazy and stop writing out their calendars? I suppose we will never know for sure.

From the coverage of events in the Middle East to the latest Hollywood movies, the media heightens our fear of the world's end, a fear that seems to be at an all-time high. Are we collectively becoming more in tune with apocalyptic dread for a reason? Maybe, but perhaps it is just more of the same end-of-the-world fear we have always had. Medieval Europeans thought the world was on the verge of ending just about every year. Their fears were justified with the Black Death, constant warfare, and no working sewers—I would want the world to end too.

God knows we fear the unknown, especially the future. This is why the Bible incorporates a large amount of prophecy. The Bible is an incredible historical document, not only because it tells the story of man's redemption through Jesus Christ, but also because it supernaturally predicts future events. A large chunk of the Bible consists of prophetic passages regarding the future. From Jesus's coming to earth, to his future second return, from the rise of empires to their collapses, the Bible has consistently revealed future events with one hundred percent accuracy.

This book is about Bible prophecies as they pertain to nations and states. I will avoid discussion of the future environmental and social woes that will befall this world and stick to the future interactions of nations. There will be no specific dates in this book. If you are looking for a date, there are a number of websites that will tell you exactly what year the Tribulation will happen, when the world will run out of oil, and when the aliens will attack. They may also predict the second coming of Elvis. Jesus plainly tells us in Matthew 24:36 that "About that day or hour no one knows, not even the angels in heaven, nor the Son, but only the Father" (NIV).

There are three main arguments I would like to pose within these pages. First, geopolitical experts' predictions mirror Biblical prophecies. Secular experts may not realize it, but their predictions regarding certain nations are eerily similar to those found in Ezekiel, Daniel, and Revelation. Recent history and current events indicate that we might be living in the end times.

The Jewish people have reestablished a nation in the Holy Land, and their neighbors don't like it. As has always been true, most of the world has turned its back on Israel. For the first time in history, old enemies of Russia, Turkey, and Iran are now best friends, just as Ezekiel foretold in the 6th century BC. As Daniel proclaimed in the court of Nebuchadnezzar, the world is hurling ever closer to one-world governance via globalization.

Second, although not mentioned specifically by name in Scripture, the role of the United States in the world's future is crucial. As the dominating force holding the geopolitical world together, the United States has inherited and improved upon the system needed for Revelation's global governance system. Western civilization has been the dominant force in the world for the past 500 years. In recent decades, the United

States has played a large role in giving the world a dominant language (English), a relentless culture (Hollywood), a vibrant currency (the dollar), and a powerful military that provides stability for the interdependent system.

Third, Jesus's return may be sooner than most people realize. More than likely it will be decades rather than centuries. Again, I do not claim to know specific dates or years in which the Rapture may occur, but demographics, technology, and fulfilled prophecies indicate that the world had better wake up.

Russian and European birthrates have fallen faster than ever. If the trend continues, Europe is in danger of becoming the next cluster of Muslim "stans." As we will see, the future rise of the Antichrist from the Western world, along with the continent's strong Greco/Roman heritage, gives it a unique role in prophetic events. Therefore, it would not make sense for Europe to succumb to an Islamic takeover. Islamic culture is neither Western nor Roman.

In addition, ancient prophecies have been fulfilled this past century. Israel has been re-gathered a second and last time before the Millennium, the world has engaged in horrific world wars, and technology has connected the globe as never before. It's time to buckle up! Jesus may be coming back soon.

Not only is the study of biblical prophecy useful in recognizing the signs of the times, but it also carries a great number of other benefits as well. It is important to remember that prophecy, although often described with detailed imagery and symbolism, represents real future events. Revelation's Millennial Kingdom is not a metaphysical, spiritual realm here on earth today but rather a future literal kingdom on earth with Christ on the throne. Just because Revelation scares faint-hearted souls does not mean it will not happen.

The physical death, burial, and resurrection of Christ was prophesied by Isaiah, Daniel, Zechariah, and many other Old Testament prophets. Daniel's Gentile Empires found in chapters 2 and 7 were authoritative empires in the Ancient world. Isaiah's prediction regarding the Persian king Cyrus's willingness to let the Jews return to Israel had a literal fulfillment. The Bible's ability to predict future events is perhaps one of the greatest witnessing tools given to Christians today.

Studying prophecy can also rescue Christians from the "daily grind." Next time you decide to read a magazine, surf the net, or watch the news, try reading through some prophetical passages instead. Revelation is guaranteed to liven up your reading life. Regarding the locust plague of the Tribulation, the Apostle John said, "and they had hair like the hair of women, and their teeth were like the teeth of lions." That is not a Lady Gaga outfit.

Spending the time to understand difficult passages will not only be rewarding intellectually but spiritually as well, for God says "Look, I am coming soon! Blessed is the one who keeps the words of the prophecy written in this scroll" (Revelation 22:7).

Geopolitics and the Bible

There will be much ado about geopolitics and international relations in this book. In fact, the majority of this book will be spent exploring the foreign policy of specific nations. Although God holds men and women individually accountable, and the acceptance of salvation is an individual rather than collective event, the Bible is clear that one day nations will be held accountable for their actions.

> In those days and at that time, when I restore the fortunes of Judah and Jerusalem, I will gather all nations and bring them down to the Valley of Jehoshaphat. There I will put them on trial for what they did to my inheritance, my people Israel, because they scattered my people among the nations and divided up my land. (Joel 3:1–2)

Christ will judge the actions of nations after the Battle of Armageddon in the valley of Jehoshaphat, also known as the Judgment of Nations. Nations who treated Israel with kindness will in turn be blessed, while nations who mistreated God's people will be cursed.

The official dictionary definition of geopolitics explains that it is "the study of the influence of such factors as geography, economics, and demography on politics, and especially of the foreign policy of a state."[1] In other words, geopolitics seeks to understand behavior and interaction between nations. Its study is helpful in understanding why North Korea cannot seem to behave, why Iran hates Israel, or why Uruguay never seems to accomplish anything as a nation (on an international level). Nevertheless, I'm sure their food is amazing.

Geopolitics is also helpful for those who attempt to predict the future in general terms. Shying away from specific people and actual dates, experts use logic, culture, and history to see trends in a nation's actions, thereby predicting how they may act in the future. For instance, it does not take a strategic expert to know that the Netherlands, a country split between gay tolerant/eco-worshipping/progressives and Sharia-loving/gay intolerant/traditional Muslims, will have a tough time holding itself together.

This process of logical guessing is known as strategic forecasting, coined by George Friedman, a modern-day geopolitical prophet of sorts. Friedman himself is quite famous for predicting geopolitical earthquakes before they happen. Although he is not always right, he is not often wrong. Imagine how right he could be if he used the Scriptures for help.

Unfortunately, neither Friedman nor any other strategic forecasters have sought the Bible in their explorations of the future until now. This book seeks to unite Bible prophecy and strategic forecasting together under one roof. Biblical strategic forecasting analyzes the potential future while using Bible prophecy as a compass. In addition to being a guide to salvation and living, the Bible is also a great strategic forecasting tool. God is right about his predictions one hundred percent of the time.

For instance, the Scripture gives us a number of geopolitical events that will happen in the future: Babylon will be rebuilt, Israel will come under attack by Russia, Iran, and their allies, and the Western world will continue to dominate globally. Additionally, this helps us to better understand the actions Iran and Russia are taking today. What we do not know is how or when this will all come to pass. That is where a keen understanding of the geopolitical landscape can play a crucial role in better understanding the prophecies of the Bible. Let us now begin to understand the intricacies of Biblical prophecy.

Part I
THE END-TIMES ROLE OF THE WEST

Chapter One

THE RISE OF WESTERN CIVILIZATION AND GLOBALIZATION

Finally, there will be a fourth kingdom, strong as iron—for iron breaks and smashes everything—and as iron breaks things to pieces, so it will crush and break all the others. Just as you saw that the feet and toes were partly of baked clay and partly of iron, so this will be a divided kingdom; yet it will have some of the strength of iron in it, even as you saw iron mixed with clay. As the toes were partly iron and partly clay, so this kingdom will be partly strong and partly brittle. And just as you saw the iron mixed with baked clay, so the people will be a mixture and will not remain united, any more than iron mixes with clay. (Daniel 2:40–43)

C hristopher Columbus was a desperate man—five weeks at sea and still no sign of land. His crew was on the verge of mutiny, and he had agreed to turn around if land was not seen in two days' time. To add to the pressure, his promises to the most powerful monarch in Europe echoed in the back of his mind. The Spanish king would be furious should Columbus fail to find a western sea route to Asia. Therefore, with three Spanish galleons, hundreds of men, and a hefty loan from the Royal Crown, Columbus had no choice but to continue into the unknown waters of the Atlantic.

Little did he know that the fate of the Western world rested upon his success or his failure. By 1492, Christendom and Islam had been at war for nearly 800 years. Beginning with Islam's swift conquest of the Middle East in the 7th century AD, Muslim armies crushed the old Christian civilizations of Egypt, Syria, and North Africa.

After 500 years of continual warfare, Spanish crusaders had finally managed in 1492 to free their own lands from Islamic rule. The last Muslim state in Spain, Grenada, fell to the conquistadores a few months prior to Columbus's voyage. These recent gains against the Muslims gave Europeans hope that they were winning the battle of civilizations.

Farther to the east, the Muslim Ottoman Empire only continued to expand. In 1453, the Ottoman Empire finally captured Constantinople, destroying what was left of the Byzantine Empire. In addition to capturing the spiritual capital of the Orthodox Church, the Ottomans had control of the eastern trade routes as well. The Christian Kingdoms of Europe were in danger of being cut off from the ancient overland trade routes to the East. Europeans would need another way to access Asian goods.

Ferdinand and Isabella, both pious Catholics, believed they were at war with Islam. Having recently exiled all Muslims from Spain, the powerful couple was not exactly inclined to negotiate with the Ottomans. Instead, they sought an alternate route, one that was hopefully faster than the Portuguese habit of sailing around the coast of Africa.

Finally, on October 11, 1492, Columbus and his crew accidentally sailed into two vast continental systems—the Americas. Not only had Columbus rescued his own ambitious future, but he had also rescued the future of Europe. For the next 300 years, Western European nations had sole access to the largest gold mine in history. Gold, silver, coffee, cocoa, timber, sugar, and a slew of other natural resources flooded the capital cities of Madrid, Lisbon, Paris, Amsterdam, and London. The Ottomans had their land routes to Asia, but the Europeans had two new continents for the taking. The discovery of the Americas gave the Europeans a considerable edge over other world civilizations.

Columbus had failed to find an eastern sea route to Asia and died a broken man. Nevertheless, history justified his discovery, as he and a handful of foolhardy Spaniards accidentally put Western Civilization on the fast track to world domination.

DESCENDANTS OF THE GRECO-ROMAN WORLD

The Western world owes much of its cultural success to its Roman and Greek ancestors. The Western world was the natural heir to the Roman one. From concepts of government to ways of thinking, Western culture imitates its predecessor.

The Roman alphabet, Julian calendar, system of republican government, and romance languages are but a few of the cultural inheritances the West received from Greece and Rome. Even the symbolism of the Roman eagle still resides in Western nations. From "American Eagle" clothing to a multitude of national flags, the eagle is a symbol of power and pride to many Western nations today.

Perhaps the most direct lineage can be seen in the West's system of government—democracy and republicanism. Democracy, originally an Athenian Greek idea, gave ancient Greek city/states the ability to run their lives as they saw fit, more so than any other political system of the day. In Athens, all free male leaders of their households could participate in government affairs. Women, slaves, and foreigners were not permitted to join in the fun, but this system was much freer than any king or emperor who had come before.

The Romans borrowed much from the Greeks, especially their democratic form of government. The Romans tweaked the system and created a form of democracy known as republicanism. This system was to last over 400 years until the Republic collapsed under the weight of imperialism.

During the 1st century BC, however, corruption began to eat away at the Republic. Wealthy individuals began purchasing elected positions, and the ideals of the Roman Republic began to sink into the Tiber River. Rival generals seized power and fought until eventually, Augustus Caesar won the greatest prize of all—Emperor of Rome. The ideas of democracy and republicanism, although stifled during the rule of the Caesars, lived on well past the fall of Rome itself. Today, over half of the world's nations profess to have a legitimate form of a republic. Although some of these nations are corrupt, they at least admire the idea of a free republic (except Russia, Iran, and maybe the city of Chicago). Most of these nations can be found in the Western World.

THE WESTERN WORLD IN SCRIPTURE

Where is this powerful Western world found in Scripture? Bible scholars

21

pinpoint both the rise of Rome and the Western world in the books of Daniel and Revelation. A study of Scripture and history will show that the Western world has created a geopolitical environment in which the Tribulation could take place today.

Most of the West's rise to prominence is seen in the book of Daniel. Daniel not only saw the rise of the Persian, Greek, and Roman Empires, but also saw the rise of Rome's descendants—the Western World. It is very likely that we are living in the high watermark of Western civilization, foreseen by Daniel over 2,500 years ago.

Daniel's Geopolitical Dreams

Daniel received two of his geopolitical prophecies through the King's dreams. Found in Daniel Chapters 2 and 7, King Nebuchadnezzar's dreams consisted of a statue made of various metals and animal-like beasts, respectively. The famous statue dream reads as follows:

> The head of the statue was made of pure gold, its chest and arms of silver, its belly and thighs of bronze, its legs of iron, its feet partly of iron and partly of baked clay. While you were watching, a rock was cut out, but not by human hands. It struck the statue on its feet of iron and clay and smashed them. Then the iron, the clay, the bronze, the silver and the gold were all broken to pieces and became like chaff on a threshing floor in the summer. The wind swept them away without leaving a trace. But the rock that struck the statue became a huge mountain and filled the whole earth. (Daniel 2:32–35)

In the remainder of the passage, Daniel explained that each metal represented a different future empire, starting from the head and working its way down to the toes in a timeline of future history. The Babylonian Empire was represented by a head of gold, while Persia was illustrated with arms of silver. These were followed by Greece with a bronze torso, and Rome with two legs of iron. The feet of this statue, consisting of iron and clay, represented the offspring of the Romans—the Western world.

The entire statue will eventually be struck and destroyed by a large rock, which represents Christ and his millennial kingdom (see Daniel 2:39–45).

Nebuchadnezzar had yet another dream. In this dream four beasts came up out of the sea. The same future empires were represented by visions. Babylon was illustrated as a "lion with the wings of an eagle." This animal was followed by a bear, a leopard, and a nasty looking iron beast with ten horns (see Daniel 7:5–7).

These beasts are again the same three kingdoms previously mentioned in Chapter 2. Daniel was visibly shaken by the fourth kingdom, and rightly so—it was frightening. God gave him a little extra explanation in the following passage.

> He gave me this explanation: 'The fourth beast is a fourth kingdom that will appear on earth. It will be different from all the other kingdoms and will devour the whole earth, trampling it down and crushing it. The ten horns are ten kings who will come from this kingdom. After them another king will arise, different from the earlier ones; he will subdue three kings. (Daniel 7:23–24)

As history indicates, every arm, leg, foot, and metal represented a specific event, kingdom, or person in history. The kingdom that came after Nebuchadnezzar's was represented by the arms of silver in the statue and in animal form as a lumbering bear. This empire was none other than Persia. Divided as they were between the Medes and the Persians, its rulers were not as powerful as Nebuchadnezzar, but they could whip up massive armies that moved slowly, yet efficiently, much like a bear.

Daniel saw two hundred years into the future for the next world empire: Alexander the Great and the Greeks. Alexander's armies, depicted as a leopard with the wings of an eagle, raced across Asia, destroying the Persian Empire in the process. The bronze metal of the Greeks represented even more dilution of power, as Alexander's empire was held together by one man. It soon fell apart after he died, only to be conquered by the final beast.

The final "iron beast" started out as Rome, but it will end in the future as something else. The Romans conquered the entire Mediterranean world. God attributes iron to the Romans because they were indeed more powerful than the earlier empires. Carthaginians, Barbarians, Greeks, and Jews were all conquered by the Roman legions.

The division of the Roman Empire by Diocletian in the 4th century AD is evidenced in Daniel's statue as "two iron legs," but it is the feet of iron and clay that present a dilemma. If the iron beast is one kingdom representing the Roman Empire, where is the Roman Empire today? After its split, the Western half fell in 476 AD, while the Eastern half lived on for another 1,000 years, until it was conquered by the Ottoman Turks. The Roman Empire today is nonexistent as a political entity. Therefore, the feet and toes cannot be directly attributed to the Roman Empire.

Many Bible scholars argue that after the legs of iron, Daniel's predictions take a long break, waiting for the feet and toes to be fulfilled in the future. This is encapsulated in the idea that Europe will become a revived Roman Empire, divided by ten European districts or kingdoms. The European-revived Roman Empire theory is faulty for two reasons.

First, Daniel clearly says the final beast "devours the whole earth." History has proven that the Romans never conquered the whole earth. In fact, they didn't even conquer the known world. Contrary to Hollywood, Spartacus and his escaped slaves had a great chance at evading the Roman legions. All they had to do was head north for about fifty miles and they would have been out of Roman territory! But what kind of movie ending would that have made? Most of the ancient world lay well outside the Roman sphere of power.

In Revelation Chapter 17, the same beast described by Daniel was also described by John. The beast with seven heads and ten horns was being ridden upon by Babylon the harlot, the future one world religion. John also described the beast as "the seven heads are seven mountains, on which the woman sits ...." It is often thought that these "seven mountains" represented the seven hills of the city of Rome. Rome, being the capital of the beast's empire, fits the "revived Roman empire" theory nicely, but prominent Bible scholar Dr. Arnold Fruchtenbaum disagrees.

He explains that many ancient cities sat on "seven hills," and, therefore, should not be solely attributed to Rome. Also, whenever the word "mountains" is used in prophetic passages, it always represents kings or kingdoms rather than a city, or more simply a hill.[1] With this in mind, the seven mountains or seven hills in Revelation cannot mean a city such as Rome.

Dr. Fruchtenbaum believes these symbols represent the end times beast's domination over the earth. "Seven mountains," or rather seven kingdoms that have dominion over the earth, will be seven of the ten remaining regions of the world that share power with the antichrist. The beast of Daniel and Revelation will not simply devour Europe, but in the guise of ten world regions or world kingdoms, the beast will "devour the whole earth."[2]

The second disagreement is geopolitical. Despite creating the European Union, Europe is still a very fragmented place and is in no position to fall under the leadership of one nation or leader. Since the fall of Rome, a number of Europeans sought to unite the continent under one rule. Mussolini even dreamed of reviving the Roman Empire. Charlemagne, Barbarossa, Napoleon, and Hitler all tried and failed to bring Europe together with devastating consequences. Eventually, the antichrist will unite Europe, but he will also unite much of the Western world behind him as well.

The antichrist will be a Western dictator. In Daniel 9:26, Daniel described the antichrist as being a descendant of the ancient Romans.

After the sixty-two "sevens," the Anointed One will be put to death and will have nothing. The people of the ruler who will come will destroy the city and the sanctuary. The end will come like a flood: War will continue until the end, and desolations have been decreed.

"The people of the ruler who will come," who destroyed Jerusalem and the sanctuary, were the Romans in 70 AD, which means that the antichrist will be someone of European or Roman descent.

The Identity of the Iron Feet

All of Daniel's gentile world empires (Babylonian, Persian, Greek, and Roman) were massive centralized governments with tremendous power. Often times, these empires used their power to create tyranny and oppression. Occasionally, there were spurts of freedom and liberty, as in the case of the Roman republic and the democracies of the Western world.

The "iron feet," or the prominence of the Western world, have been blessed with a greater degree of freedom than all of its predecessors. Although the West has seen its share of violent dictators, it has also experienced some of the freest societies in history.

Daniel explained that the iron feet were part of the fourth kingdom of iron, yet different, as it had "some strength of iron, but was mixed with clay," and "the people will be a mixture and will not remain united, any more than iron mixes with clay" (Daniel 2:42-43). Perhaps what made the iron feet divisive were the many different types of peoples, cultures, and governments of the Western world.

The divided iron/clay feet of the statue, although connected to the legs, represent a new era of history, one that bridges the gap between the fall of the old Roman Empire and the future era of the ten-toed Tribulation kingdom. The feet represent many divided nations and loyalties. These nations were strong in the fact that they had inherited much from the Roman Empire, but they were weak in their lack of unity. The feet of iron and clay in Daniel's statue undoubtedly represent the era of Western dominance.

Western Civilization's Ascent to Power

After the fall of Rome, the future of Western civilization looked dire. Barbaric tribes, Asian horsemen, and Persian kings were all competing for power amidst the vacuum left behind from the Roman collapse. It was indeed a dark time for Europe, as poverty, disease, violence, and death were a way of life for millions of Europeans.

Despite constant warfare and the depressingly low life spans of Europeans, however, they were slowly developing institutions that would help them in the future. Monarchs were organizing Europe's vast feudal fiefdoms and territories into larger kingdoms, with France, Spain, and England being prime examples. These kingdoms would eventually centralize power and create the institutions necessary for powerful nation/states to thrive. National identity, centralized governments, and standing armies would eventually bring Europeans back into the game.

Meanwhile, Europe's neighbors were flourishing. Mongol and Tatar horsemen dominated much of Asia, the Middle Kingdom of China was still the center of the East, and India continued to thrive. The Medieval Period was also the Golden Age of Islam. The Muslims achieved cultural dominance for a number of centuries. From Cordoba to Baghdad, Arab societies studied astronomy and geometry, wrote poetry and literature, and unlike their European neighbors, bathed regularly.

By 1453 AD, it looked as if the Muslims would continue to be the dominant civilization, as they had just conquered the ancient Byzantine city of Constantinople. In addition to cutting off trade to the East, the Muslim Ottoman Empire captured one of the greatest Christian cities in the world. In regular Islamic fashion, the Muslims renamed the pillar of Orthodox architecture, the Hagia Sofia Cathedral, to the Aya Sofia Mosque.

Out of necessity, Europeans began to reconnect with their ancient Greco-Roman roots. The need for innovation and technology created a thirst for knowledge, stirring European inventors, scholars, and mathematicians to rekindle their fascinations with the works of Plato, Archimedes, and Pythagoras. Miraculously, a number of movements soon began taking form in Western Europe.

The 15th century gave rise to a great machine—the printing press—which bore a great revolution—the Renaissance. Over the next 300 years, the Renaissance in turn spawned four more great movements across Europe: the Reformation, the Age of Exploration, the Scientific Revolution, and the Enlightenment.

The Printing Press, created in 1440 by Johannes Gutenberg, was perhaps the one invention that allowed Western civilization to dominate for the next 500 years. The printing press was the 15th century equivalent of the Internet. Across Europe, Bibles, science books, history texts, and children's stories were soon spewing forth from printing presses. Europeans copied everything from scriptural commentaries to medical treatises, and even the latest tactics in firearm training. The first modern firearm, introduced in 1415, was handy as well. Despite still being relatively poor and weak, the Europeans now held two great advantages—the keys to knowledge and power.

Other civilizations eventually caught on to the printing press and the firearm, but it was too late. European literacy rates skyrocketed and new inventions were developed. Portuguese and Spanish explorations spawned the need for new ship building techniques, including the ocean-crossing frigate. Invaluable inventions such as the compass and astrolabe (forerunner of the sextant) enabled European explorers to sail into the unknown. The earth was round again.

The Age of Exploration ushered in European sea power as well. By Columbus's discovery of the New World in 1492, the Portuguese had already sailed around Africa, establishing trade routes with India, China, and the Far East. Soon after, French, Dutch, and English ports began popping up along African, Asian, and American sea routes. Europeans were quickly becoming the masters of the seas.

Despite advances in science and education, the 16th and 17th centuries saw continuous warfare during the wars of the Reformation between Catholics and Protestants. Nonetheless, this constant warfare bred competition. Much like the space race between the USSR and the USA, the Europeans constantly tried to out-invent each other. From firearms to cannons, Europeans of this period were constantly reconfiguring the best ways to kill each other.

Even so, Western dominance was not an outright conclusion. The Ottoman Empire of the Middle East was still incredibly powerful. They controlled most of the Middle East and North Africa, and, as late as 1683, nearly captured the Austrian capital of Vienna. They did, however, miss the technology boat. Ottoman cannons were outdated. Their ships could not counter the size and speed of Western warships. The dreaded Janissaries, an elite fighting force of slave soldiers, whom in past centuries were the most feared army in the world, eventually gave ground to more effective Western armies.

After 1,000 years of plague, war, and hardship, Western civilization was once again the dominant force on the planet. By the 18th century, French, Spanish, Portuguese, Dutch, and English colonies enveloped the Western Hemisphere, and they were making significant headway in Africa, India, and Southeast Asia. European warships controlled the sea lanes, and other civilizations could do little about it. By the late 19th century, the feet of Daniel's statue were walking wherever they chose.

Globalization

After the discovery of the New World and the opening of Asian and African markets, Europeans soon began to realize that their actions abroad led to consequences at home. The Spanish were the first to discover this concept. The Spanish conquistadores stripped so much gold and silver from the New World that they over-burdened their economy with inflation. Embroiling themselves in nearly every conflict of the 17th century did not help their economic woes either.

From 1492-1776, millions of Europeans and Africans migrated to the New World. Historian John Darwin explains that these massive movements set up inter-Atlantic connections and trade routes crucial to the development of a global economy.[3] Along with Atlantic sea routes, the industrial revolution further expanded globalization, enabling Europeans to get more goods to distant markets more quickly.[4] It was possible for a French merchant to sell his wares not only in France, but also to Sioux Indians on the American Plains, Berbers in the deserts of North Africa, or Chinese in the city of Shanghai.

After the defeat of Napoleon in 1815, the British Empire became the de facto leader of the Western world. They were by far the wealthiest and, with the British Royal Navy, had the best means of protecting the waterways. According to Darwin, the British desired above all else to keep free trade safe. The plan was to integrate as much of the globe as possible with trade allegiances.[5]

Just "as iron mixes with clay," so too did the Western powers mix—badly. With the rise of Germany and Italy in the late 19th century, the British concept of MAD was blown out of the water with two world wars and another Cold War after that. Soon, a very different economic system arose, one that was in every way opposed to capitalism—communism. The globe was still interconnected, but it was hindered by the stress of the Cold War alliances. It was not until the fall of Communism in 1990 that the Eastern Bloc countries were fully able to join the world markets again.

The fall of the Soviet Union also gave the other superpower, the United States of America, a chance not only to spread capitalism but also democracy, another key component of Western Civilization, to the Eastern bloc.[6] Soon after the fall, Soviet satellite nations embraced democracy and capitalism with abandon. Even China betrayed its Communist ideology for the financial success capitalism would bring.

GLOBALIZATION AND THE TRIBULATION

The 16th century began a worldwide trend of interdependence. The world began to shrink, linking nearly every nation together in one giant web of economic necessity. Since the fall of the Soviet Union in 1991, globalization has transformed the world. Today, Philippine teenagers wait in line to hear British rock stars, while Brazilian teenagers wait in line to see Australian movie stars. The airline industry spans continents in hours, while the Internet spans continents in seconds. Uprisings in the Middle East, earthquakes in Japan, and volcanoes in Iceland are no longer regional issues since they impact every country on the planet. Like it or not, we are a global community.

Foretold in the book of Daniel, the nations of the Western world not only colonized a great expanse of the globe, but also created the trappings of a global economy, shrinking the world and setting it on a course to globalization. The Western world has also unwittingly created the perfect global control system, a worldwide economic interdependence that the antichrist will exploit in the future.

Perhaps even more important to future events has been the formation of the United States. What began as a string of British colonies at the edge of the world eventually became the most powerful Western nation in history, dwarfing even the power of the Roman Empire. Contrary to popular belief, the United States may have a crucial role to play in the future as it keeps the global system alive and well until events in the Tribulation begin to take shape.

Chapter Two

THE END-TIMES ROLE OF THE UNITED STATES

"He gave me this explanation: 'The fourth beast is a fourth kingdom that will appear on earth. It will be different from all the other kingdoms and will devour the whole earth, trampling it down and crushing it. (Daniel 7:23)

Will the United States sink into a massive sinkhole in the future? Will it get hit by a meteor the size of Texas? To be honest, anything is possible if God wants America out of the picture. A tsunami the size of Ireland could hit the east coast tomorrow for all we know. But if God had wanted the United States out of the picture, he had many opportunities to do so.

Right from the start, America could have been destroyed before it began. Their declaration from Britain in 1776 could have been a disaster. The British military was the most powerful on earth and the British economy vast. Meanwhile, the American colonists were little more than farmers, lawyers, and tradesmen. Yet with God's blessing, America eventually won her independence.

The British tried again a generation later, blockading ports, sinking ships, and even burning down Washington, D.C. America won again, however, and it was the last time a foreign power tried to invade the young nation.

Napoleon had ambitions for a French Empire in America, but a small slave revolt in the tiny French colony of Haiti changed all his plans. After the Haitian revolt, Napoleon had no choice but to sell to America the French lands referred to as the Louisiana Territory. Even when a devastating Civil War rattled the country to the core, America came out the better for it, providing freedom and equality for all its citizens.

Today, many Americans fret over the threat of inflation, terrorist attacks, or natural disasters. It has been a common assumption amongst evangelicals that the United States will disappear before the end times. The scenarios are many—a series of nuclear attacks by terrorists, a debilitating plague, or a crippling civil war—for the fall of the United States. Alec Baldwin could get elected president and install a utopian socialism run by Hollywood elites. That would definitely be the end of America.

Other than fear, the reasons behind the America-is-going-to-be-destroyed hysteria is the fact that there is no specific mention of America in the Bible like there is of Israel, Iran, or Egypt. Using the same reasoning, there is no mention of Icelanders, I-pads, or high-speed trains either, yet we know they will be a continued presence.

More than likely, the United States will continue to play an instrumental role in creating and sustaining the necessary economic and geopolitical environment for the "latter days." For those who worry about the destruction of America, perhaps this chapter will alleviate any future panic attacks.

Today America is the undisputed leader of Western civilization. If the feet of Daniel's statue represent Western civilization, then may I submit that the United States of America are the socks giving the world a layer of protection and stability from blisters and such? Its military is unrivaled, its financial stability as the world leader is resilient, and its cultural impact may be the most relentless in history.

It pains me to use the term, given my American love for limited government, but the United States truly is the first "global empire" in history. But America is nothing like the empires of the past. This one happens to be a republic with constitutional freedoms guaranteed to its citizens. In the latter half of the 20th century, the United States never went to war for plunder or territory but rather to keep stability. Much time, money, and blood was spent rescuing other nations from Nazis, Communists, and radical Islamists.

America has become the headmaster of the world. George Friedman calls it the unintended empire, as our policies "shape the lives of people on every continent."[1] Zbigniew Brzezinski, a former White House advisor, states that "Washington, D.C. is the first global capital in the history of the world," since it is the center of global power and decision-making.[2]

When President Obama was elected in 2008, there were tingles running down the legs of not only MSNBC host Chris Matthews, but also a large number of Europeans as well. Many Europeans were excited to see the new American president and visited his European speeches in droves. Why? They understand that the President of the USA is the de facto leader of the world. When the President of the United States makes decisions, it affects the entire globe.

Today, America's strategic plans are simple—keep stability. American foreign policy seeks to preserve the waterways and to keep regional powers limited.[3] By acting as the stabilizing agent in the world, America is guaranteed political clout in nearly every continent. In addition, ancient regional rivalries are kept at bay by the threat of American intervention.

Critics would argue that America has no right to be the "world's policeman." Ron Paul spends more time critiquing America's role as world police than he does running for president. Sorry, Representative Paul, world's policeman may sound presumptuous and arrogant, but America has been thrust into that position whether she likes it or not. Should the world's policeman take an extended holiday or retire, chaos would break out. Imagine a kindergarten class without a teacher, or an Eminem concert without security.

American hegemony did not occur overnight. It was more or less inherited from the British Empire after the world wars and handed over by the Soviets after the Cold War. After WWII, the British lost the desire, and to a large extent the ability to hold the global system together. Europe was in shambles, and Russia had rejected the free market, leaving the United States as the sole protector of the global system.

The United States was fortunate enough to have barely been touched by the wars, while other world leaders experienced the destruction of their infrastructures and economies. Uncle Sam and his Marshall Plan were there to pick up the pieces. Designed to rebuild Europe and Japan and protect them from Communism, the Marshall Plan paid a hefty fee for stability. Having the responsibility of rebuilding Western Europe, the Americans had a few demands—access to all strategic waterways and ports of the former British and French Empires. The British happily ceded them over, but the French responded reluctantly since they were desperate to offset the growing menace of Communism.

After the fall of the Soviet Union, however, the Americans were the only legitimate superpower presiding over the global system, which now included former communist states. It had access to and control of all strategic waterways (guaranteeing economic stability),[4] command of all Western forces under NATO, and the military power to back up their demands whenever and wherever.

MILITARY

For the five people in the world who doubt US military hegemony, there are some telling statistics. In the first decade of the 21st century, the United States has routinely spent forty percent of the world's annual estimated military costs. In other words, of the entire globe's military spending, the USA is responsible for forty percent. If one were to combine every naval vessel from every nation and match them up against the US Navy, they still wouldn't match up in number or firepower.[5]

The worlds most advanced weapons systems are still built in the US, not China. From the atom bomb to the stealth helicopter, America has led the way in the latest weapons technology. The best other nations can hope for is to bribe, steal, and beg for American military secrets, thereby copying American ingenuity.

If sheer firepower and technology is not enough evidence for military superiority, the American experience has bred a country destined for conquest. From the violent escape from Britain to the beaches of Normandy, Americans have been victorious in every war they have fought (Vietnam being the exception as a tactical tie and a strategic retreat).

America has experienced fighting and winning drastically different wars as well. From the asymmetrical warfare against Native American tribes to massive head-on assaults in the world wars, America has triumphed. If this is sounding like an American pep rally, it is.

As the protector of stability, one of America's responsibilities is to react quickly to any global unrest. The only superpower in history with the ability to strike anywhere on the globe in a matter of hours is the United States. Respect and fear of America's military keeps regional rivals under control. It keeps North Korea from invading South Korea, Iran from invading Iraq, and even Russia from invading Poland. To an extent, it even keeps Michigan from invading Ohio during college football season.

The one military that comes closest to stacking up with the US is technically not even a real military or country but rather a unified Europe. Although they may be semi-united financially, the cultural/historical barriers to military unification would render this situation impossible. In fact, when cooperating together, the United States and Western Europe represent, as Brzezinski says, "the core of global power and wealth."[6]

China and Japan are trying to increase their military capabilities, and their gains have been promising; but for many years neither will be able to challenge the other, let alone the United States. Russia is rapidly increasing its military production but they are running out of time, demographically speaking. There is no other nation with the will or the means to challenge American supremacy on the battlefields or in the banks.

THE US ECONOMY

Despite the setbacks of the 2008 recession, the United States is still incredibly powerful. When the US economy flourishes, so does the rest of the world. For one, the US is the center of gravity for all trade.[7] Europe's center of gravity is the Atlantic Ocean while Asia's is the Pacific. They all hinge on trade with the United States. Asian countries especially rely on America to protect the sea-lanes and buy their goods. [8]

Secondly, the United States owns the world's only reserve currency.[9] In recent years both Russia and China have whined about America's reserve currency. Despite all their yapping, no country in the world would trust China or Russia to protect the world's reserve currency. Should the world markets collapse, the United States has a bit more cushion than everyone else.

Contrary to popular belief, Scripture never indicates that the world will eventually have one currency. The antichrist forces all upon the earth to take his mark in order to buy and sell, but Revelation does not specify as to what currency they may be using.[10] Nonetheless, the dollar has become the world's most important currency.

There has been much anxiety regarding the falling value of the US dollar and economy, and rightly so. Gold prices have soared, stocks have fallen, and road rage has increased. (I'm sure that's involved somehow). Our recent credit downgrade is also troubling. Despite the woes of the American dollar, there is no other dominant currency waiting in the wings to replace it.

Consider the Chinese dragon, for instance. As a teacher, I will hear the occasional class clown utter a foolish comment such as "China's economy is so much greater than ours." Or, "China has a billion people in their army." As the fervor escalates, more and more students chime in with, "Chinese schools are better, their food is better, their basketball players are better, etcetera." It is also common to hear the media making these same disparaging comments.

The Chinese worship reaches a sickening crescendo as students realize most of their clothes are also made in China. Some students even begin texting their parents, asking for a one-way ticket to Beijing. My response is, "Blah. Try living as a Chinese citizen for six months. You would come back craving hamburgers (not made from dog or cat), Internet access free of government control, and NFL football. All the while you would be praising the American freedoms you have always taken for granted. Does China even have a show like *American Idol*?"

Here is also something to keep in mind if one suffers from China envy: the US economy is three times that of China, as well as twenty-five percent of the entire world's economy.[11] Yes, the Chinese government holds 2.5 trillion dollars of US debt.[12] This is an astounding number on the surface but not as threatening as it seems. The US is China's number one consumer, therefore China needs the United States to continue buying its products. Should the Chinese demand payment and force us to default on the loans, there would be devastating consequences not only for America but for China as well. Strategist Joseph Nyse, Jr. exclaims,

"China could bring the US to it's knees, but would in effect bring China to it's ankles."[13]

In addition to being shackled to the US economy, Friedman notes that China also has one billion people in poverty, a rather large elephant in the room of Chinese policy makers.[14] At some point in the future the Chinese government will be faced with a huge dilemma—how to lift a billion people out of poverty while sustaining economic growth. All the free bicycles and rice in the world could not accomplish such a feat.

The dollar itself is quickly becoming the world's currency. The Russians and Chinese dream of creating a new global currency, but they have nothing to put forward. Neither the Ruble nor the Yuan have the stamina. As Economist Benjamin Cohen puts it, the dollar is the number one monetary unit for transactions between nations, "the most favored vehicle for currency trading."[15]

Will the next world currency please stand up? Is it the mighty Euro? Cohen does not think so, and explains that the 2008 crisis was the Euro's last chance to challenge the dollar.[16] When the crisis exploded, businesses and corporations did not flock to the Euro for stability but rather to the dollar.[17] Although the Euro is the world's second most prolific currency, it does not have the stamina to keep up with the dollar.

The European Union was initially designed for two purposes: to counter growing Japanese and American economic power, and to further integrate Europe into a community. Since 2008 Europe has been edging closer to division rather than unity.

The United Kingdom is closer to the United States culturally and economically.[18] Germany has been shifting closer to the Russians out of necessity. France is suspicious of the new German-Russian relationship. Spain, Portugal, and Italy are on the verge of economic ruin, while Greece continues to set itself on fire every couple of years. The ambiguous, divided nature of the European Union will continually be a hindrance if they want the world's dominating currency.[19]

This leaves Japan. Does Japan have what it takes to overcome US economic superiority? No. They had their shot in the 1980s but ran into the logistical issues of continued economic growth. Besides, the US GDP on average is 3.5 times larger than Japan's.[20] American natural resources, still largely untapped, are vast, while Japan's island nation must continually import most of its resources. The US population is holding steady while Japan's is suffering from the same rapid population decline as Europe.

Critics may claim that although the US has the dominant currency, it lacks in other areas of an economy. Really. How about investments? In 2009, the United States was responsible for 22.5 percent of all foreign investments in the world.[21] How about research? The US spends more on research than the next seven nations following it combined.[22] Maybe Americans lack in creativity? The citizens of the United States held 80,000 patents last year, more than the rest of the world's nations combined.[23] The US also leads the world in information technology, nano technology, and biotechnology as well.[24] The US has little to fear from rival economies.

What does economic superiority do for the strategic future of the United States? It gives the US an incredible advantage should an alliance of nations seek to destroy, or more likely, knock the US off the hill. This scenario is also unlikely, as it is now in the interests of all nations to protect United States national security. As Brzezinski explains, "Globalization would not be politically powerful without a national base."[25] That base is the USA, and without it, the entire global system would collapse.

Furthermore, nations who have benefited from globalization would be hesitant to join in on any attacks against the US. Globalization provides nations with open markets, the opportunity for economic growth, and the free flow of trade and capital.[26] What regional or national leader would willingly commit political and economic suicide by attacking the US? Okay, besides Kim Jong Il, or Mahmoud Ahmadenijad. It seems that the United States has all the cards for now, including the Ace of culture.

THE CULTURE CONQUEROR

Perhaps more powerful than its military or economy is the American culture; the forefront of Western culture. Just as its Roman predecessor did, American culture dominates the earth. From political concepts of republicanism and individual rights, to Google and Hollywood, the United States's culture reaches far and wide. But no cultural trait has dominated more so than the language of English.

Speaking the language of the dominant superpower has always been a wise move. It opens new doors to economic and political power, and also enables countries to know when to duck or run for cover as well. Today, over four billion people speak English fluently.[27] The other 2.5 billion are either in diapers, hiding in caves, or trying to learn. Social scientist Robert McCrum explains that English has become an international communication tool on the Internet, as well as the language of business and diplomacy.[28]

The language of English, a small branch of the Germanic language tree, survived a thousand years of invasions, plagues, and warfare thanks to the plucky resilience of the English people. Having been a colony of England, the United States naturally chose the language of her mother country.

As McCrum explains, the English language received a huge international power boost when the primary language of two out of the six members of the UN Security Council (the UK and the US) was English.[29] The world's first international radio broadcasts from the BBC were played in English, as well as the world's first TV shows.[30] Basically, those living in non-English speaking countries either had to understand English, or find someone who could.

Speaking a language other than English was not a problem for many. By the advent of TV and radio, many people across the globe already spoke English, thanks to the width and breadth of the British Empire. "The sun never set on the British Empire," as the adage goes, until the British Empire retired and left her fortune to the Americans. Nonetheless, millions of non-English speakers learned English under the rule of the Crown.

If TV hadn't cemented English's dominance over the communication world, the Internet would have. Having been created by English speakers, English soon became the *lingua franca* of the Internet.[31] Computer programming software was created in English, using the English alphabet. Anyone who wanted to improve upon computer technology had to first learn rudimentary English.[32] With staggering numbers, English dominates the Internet today, as ninety-six percent of all e-commerce websites were started in English, and seventy percent of all websites ever made originated in the United States.[33] English has cemented itself into the lives of every human on the globe.

As if the Internet were not enough of an English language spreading tool, British and American music and movie industries finish the job. Thanks to globalization, Miley Cyrus sells more CDs overseas than in the United States. Does she sing her concerts in Spanish? No. English speakers also dominate the charts. American and British bands travel the globe for months on end, singing their ditties in good 'ole English.

The American TV and movie industry is a megalith in its own right. Eighty percent of the world's movie industry originates in Hollwood.[34] Even the old French culture warrior must bow to the US movie industry, as sixty percent of its own box office revenues come from American made movies.[35]

Besides religion and history, what typically makes up one's culture is language, music, technology, art, entertainment, government, food and beverage, clothing, and hobbies, to name a few. Hmm, what are some cultural traits dominating the world today?

LANGUAGE:	English
MUSIC:	MTV (in at least six continents)
TECHNOLOGY:	I-pads, Kindles, and Stealth choppers
ARTS AND ENTERTAINMENT:	Hollywood
GOVERNMENTS:	Democracy
FOOD:	McDonalds
BEVERAGE:	Starbucks
CLOTHING:	Jeans
HOBBIES:	complaining about America (both a foreign and domestic hobby)

Globalization can create a sense of anti-Americanism, resentment from other Westernized cultures, or outright hostility from more traditional ones. Traditional cultures are coming into positive contact with the likes of Taylor Swift, but they also see the negative trends of Hollywood such as Charlie Sheen. Just as Roman inventions and way of life were so enticing for conquered societies, so too is the Western way of life. A Norwegian scholar coined it perfectly, "Empire by invitation."[36]

In the outset of the 21st century, it seems as if the United States reigns supreme over the earth. Its military supports the international financial system, which is heavily fortified by the dollar and communicated in English. In addition, the arrival of radio, TV, and the Internet has only solidified America's cultural hold on the minds of young people across the globe. As strategic forecaster George Friedman explains, "Power like this doesn't end except by war"[37] (or by the hand of God).

THE UNITED STATES AND THE END TIMES

"Wait a minute," some of you may be saying. "This sounds more like a history, sociology, and geography lesson all wrapped in one!" What is the importance of globalization to the end times? In John's Revelation, the antichrist's Tribulation kingdom is a megalithic, centralized, hyper-power with absolute control over the world. Daniel explained that this beastly kingdom would control and devour the whole earth. As indicated from Daniel's statue, world history goes something like this:

I.   Golden Babylonian rule (612 BC-539 BC)
II. Silver Persian rule (539-332 BC)
III. Bronze Greek rule (332 BC-146 BC)
IV. Iron Roman rule (146 BC- 476 AD, and 1453 AD)
V.   Iron and Clay Rule of Western civilization (1492- present)
VI. Iron and Clay rule of the Ten kingdoms of the earth (future)

Daniel explained that after the ten kingdoms of the earth (toes) are put in place, the antichrist will first topple three of the toes, and eventually take over all of the little piggies, one by one.

43

HE GAVE ME THIS EXPLANATION: 'The fourth beast is a fourth kingdom that will appear on earth. It will be different from all the other kingdoms and will devour the whole earth, trampling it down and crushing it. The ten horns are ten kings who will come from this kingdom. After them another king will arise, different from the earlier ones; he will subdue three kings. (Daniel 7:23–24)

The kings Daniel refers are three actual kings of the ten world kingdoms, or, as I like to call them, "administrative districts." Bible scholar John Phillips explains that the antichrist will accomplish what Nimrod could not: uniting the world under one godless, centralized government,[38] but only for a time.

Logistically speaking, what might a world dictator need in order to control the globe, if only for a little while? He would need overwhelming military superiority, a common unifying language, a dominant currency, access to the best technology, the ability to track everyone on the globe, a top-rate communication tool, and an interdependent global economy. Sound familiar?

The United States has created and sustained a global system perfectly suited for an end-times scenario. Only instead of Republicans or Democrats at the helm of power, it will be a satanic regime that will make Hitler's Nazis look like The Wiggles.

Before the antichrist makes his move on the world, a few shakeups need to occur. Besides the world eventually dividing into ten districts, the United States will need to be brought on board. Secondly, Russia and its allies must be destroyed by God as they invade the nation of Israel.

As Daniel explained in two of his visions, the end-times government will initially break into ten pieces as it tries to achieve a global government. Are we sure this is not Ban Ki Moon or Kofi Annan dreaming this? Daniel Chapter 2 indicates "ten toes," while Chapter 7 speaks of the end-times beast having "ten horns." Revelation also speaks of "ten horns" atop the global beast. As Dr. Fruchtenbaum explained in his commentary, *Footsteps of the Messiah*, the ten horns and toes of Daniel and Revelation do not refer simply to Europe, but to the world.[39]

The drive for global governance has been upon us for almost one hundred years. It is the progressive's utopian dream, a world united under a common governing body of nations and eco-socialism. Somewhere Woodrow Wilson is jumping for joy.

Americans love their independence and sovereignty, but as indicated by the effects of globalization, even American sovereignty has been threatened by the shrinking globe. Get-togethers at the UN nowadays consist of schemes bent on taking American money and meting it out to weaker, poorer nations. There has been a gathering argument against American dominance over the global system. If a democratic US resides over a truly global system, should not more of the globe's nations have a say in it, democratically speaking?[40]

As pressure builds on the US to give up some decision making power, American presidents may oblige the lesser powers-that-be. Just as Moses was inclined to spread the burden of power to chosen elders, America may do the same with the elders of the nations. With American oversight and approval, of course, the world will one day be carved into ten administrative districts. The US will still be the granddaddy of them all, but these ten districts will develop their own resources and power as well. The American Ten-District Approval Act is only one of a number of possible scenarios.

The bottom line, according to Scripture, however, is that the world will be divided amongst ten powers, or kingdoms, with or without the United States's help. There is much wisdom in dividing the world. First, it would help to organize the supply of energy, food, and water. Secondly, a division of ten districts would do little to offset the global system already in place; in fact, it may even foster healthy competition between the districts. Only two regions stand in the way of a completely peaceful transfer to the world's ten districts—Russia and the Middle East. Both will be covered in future chapters.

WILL AMERICA BE DESTROYED?

If God wills it, America will sink to the bottom of the sea, but according to the grand scheme of things, the destruction scenario is highly unlikely.

A great number of experts agree that should the United States be destroyed by a combination of war, disease, or natural disasters, the entire globe would fall into chaos. Just as globalization holds the world together, the United States holds globalization together. Socks, remember?

Should the US suddenly be destroyed, a number of paralyzing events would ensue. First, every ancient grudge held at bay by US military power would be unleashed. Iran would not hesitate to stake its claim on the Middle East, thereby signaling a response from Israel. This would in turn trigger a regional meltdown in the world's energy supply depot. China may decide to invade Taiwan, North Korea may invade South Korea, and Pakistan and India may finally nuke each other. Who knows what Russia would do? Al Qaeda, if it still exists, would be jumping for joy in their caves. The list continues as rival powers would seek to grab as much of the world as they could.

After global political meltdown comes global energy meltdown. Wars would trigger an energy crisis unparalleled in modern history. A gas shortage is not only bad for pizza deliverers but also for farmers and truckers as well. When the tractors run out of gas, the people run out of food. Global energy crisis would equal global starvation. Satellite communications, Internet, and other basic services would be rendered useless for a time. The stock markets would crash, international trade would halt, and the world would be beggared to a local bartering system once again.

The collapse of the US would indeed signal a global apocalypse, but much too soon. As the Scriptures indicate, global alignments do not foreshadow this doomsday scenario. For one, Ezekiel's prophecies indicate that the West will see a growing challenge to its supremacy from the East, namely Russia and its allies. What would be left of Western power without the United States? What would be left of the world if everyone were fighting over the last cheeseburger?

Additionally, in order to control the planet, the eventual end-times antichrist would need state of the art technology, undisturbed by a pre-Tribulation global catastrophe. Revelation Chapter 13 indicates that the antichrist, forced all people, great and small, rich and poor, free and slave, to receive a mark on their right hands or on their foreheads, so that they could not buy or sell unless they had the mark, which is the name of the beast or the number of its name. (Revelation 13:16–17)

Does this sound like medieval chicken bartering? Control over the entire earth's economy would require the best technologies available, ranging from imprinting credit numbers into the skin to tracking transactions online. Furthermore, without the necessary energy supplies, how could the antichrist back up any of his demands? "Take my number or else! Just as soon as I get my horsemen together, take a row boat across the Atlantic, and ride my cavalry to the middle of America (on an empty stomach because there's no food), you will be in trouble." Modern technology, including modern transportation, communications, and credit systems must still be present during the Tribulation. If the United States were to disappear overnight, so too would the global technological system that took over 500 years to build.

Without America in charge, the prophecies of Revelation would indeed have a more difficult time coming to fulfillment. First, another Western power would have to take the helm where the United States left off, a nation with the same Western/Roman heritage that could counter Russia's power. The Bible is pretty clear about the antichrist and the end-times system being a Western/Roman entity. Would Britain or France be able to lead the world? Australia? None have the capacity to stabilize and eventually control the world, nor the ability to quickly build their populations and military powers.

Secondly, assuming the global system falls apart without the United States, how will the antichrist have "power over the whole earth?" Without a global system in place to easily conquer, or a powerful Western military to use, the antichrist would not be able to achieve world domination. The United States, by all logical accounts, is here to stay.

If the United States is not destroyed, how could it justify allowing the antichrist to take over, what with our Judeo-Christian heritage and

200 million Christians and all? For the sake of argument, it is entirely possible that the United States of the future looks nothing like the America we know today. In fact, elder generations would argue the same about today's America compared to the one fifty years ago. America is great because God has blessed it. For nearly 200 years America has called itself a Christian nation, but even with the presence of so many Christians, the godly fabric of society has begun its tearing. The sanctity of marriage and life have been under flagrant attack since the 1960s. Atheism has increased tenfold as well. According to the 2008 American Religious Identification Survey, a full fifteen percent of Americans claim to be agnostic or atheist, while twenty-four percent claim to have "no religion." In 2008, the newly elected President of the United States proudly proclaimed that America is "no longer a Christian nation."

God has been taken out of school, government, and healthcare. Ever try praying in school, especially as a teacher? In 2009 a Florida principal-athletic director faced trial and prison time for praying before a school luncheon. Evidently the ACLU heard his prayers just after God did and pressed charges against him for "espousing religious beliefs and trying to convert students."[41]

No wonder MTV tried to air a TV series called *Skins*, an explicit show revolving around the sex lives of underaged teenagers. Yuck. The entertainment industry over the past forty years has worked hard to make sexual freedom (especially same-sex and outside of marriage) seem trendy and hip. Is it any wonder divorce rates and infidelity are at an all time high? Porn addictions are just the tip of the iceberg; imagine what will happen culturally when the Holy Spirit is removed from the land.

For being a nation founded on Christian principles, it's hard to find a solid Christian in government. Nearly all of the founding fathers were Christians of some denomination or another. Even self-professed deists like Thomas Jefferson and Ben Franklin were often quoted supporting the need for God in America's government. Congress was opened with prayer and Bibles were distributed in Congress. Today, however, attacks on the Ten Commandments, prayer, and the display of Christianity in the public sphere are bolder than ever.

It is even evident in our elected officials. In 2011, New York Democratic US congressman Anthony Weiner had an embarrassing scandal and was forced to resign. This is typical of about eight to ten congressmen and women each year, but his crime was a little different than most. Weiner exposed his privates to a number of women on Twitter via his Congressional account. Not one, not two, but at least six women came out with new positions and poses sent by the congressman. Indecent exposure happened to be the congressman's downfall, but this is not the saddest part of the story. A majority of his constituents wanted him to stay! Imagine George Washington riding around the Virginia countryside in the buff. What would the founders have done?

Perhaps America's gravest sin of all is abortion. The widespread killing of children in the womb grew ever more popular after the infamous Roe v. Wade Supreme Court ruling in the 1970s. According to the Pro-Life Foundation, some forty-eight million children have been aborted in the United States alone since Roe v. Wade.[42]

After the Rapture of Christ's church in the future, God will allow the tide of Tribulation to wash over the planet. With that, the greatest Christian nation in history will cease to be Christian and, sadly, will join the antichrist.

AMERICAN ANTICHRIST?

With the societal decline (accelerated by the Rapture) in full tow, it is possible to see America undergo a significant shift, not only culturally but strategically. America may one day change from a benign superpower to an aggressive, expansionist power. Should America fall into the hands of a charismatic, authoritarian leader, the focus could change quickly.

The Bible does not specify a particular country from which the antichrist will come. But an understanding of American geopolitics and a rational argument for America's existence in the end can give credence to the possibility that the antichrist might come from the United States.

If God's plan is to have the United States at hand as a stabilizer until the Tribulation, one could assume that the United States would go into the Tribulation along with the rest of the nations. Unlike Israel and Iran,

America is not mentioned specifically in Scripture, but neither are Brazil, Great Britain, France, Australia, India, as well as a whole slew of nations outside of the Middle East.

As evidenced by America's role as the global stabilizer, the United States's sudden departure would be too devastating. Global wars, energy crises, and economic collapse could potentially send the world into the Dark Ages indefinitely.

If the United States does continue into the Tribulation, one must assume that it will quickly be taken over by the antichrist, as it is part of the Western world. As Revelation detailed, the antichrist will topple three kings or leaders before he eventually takes over the earth. For the antichrist to successfully conquer the world, he would need to subdue or have the blessing of the United States.

Americans have never taken kindly to dictators conquering the world, let alone the United States, so why would America ever allow this geopolitical disaster to happen? As in the days before the fall of the Roman Republic, so it might be in the last days of the American one. Political factions and upstart leaders may drive the nation to war. In the waning days of the Roman Republic, rival generals and senators dragged its citizens into endless civil wars until one leader came out unscathed; Augustus Caesar. By the time of Augustus's ascendance, Roman citizens were so tired of conflict they had forgotten the meaning of freedom. After 400 years of freedom, they simply gave up their power to an autocratic emperor. Does freedom for safety sound familiar?

It is also possible that by the time the antichrist takes power, America will have been significantly weakened and therefore easier to conquer. There is no end to the doomsday scenarios currently rotating on cable channels. From natural disasters to terrorist plots, Americans morbidly analyze ways in which their country could get crushed. America could be annihilated, but this would mean that another Western derived nation would have to replace America as the world's Western police. That is a job for which Europe has neither the stomach nor the muscle. If America is no longer the global stabilizer, it must be replaced by another Western power.

Given the power of the United States today, the replacement scenario would take decades, if not centuries to occur. Because of the time issue, one must assume that the "America destroyed and replaced by another Western power" theory does not make sense.

Without the backing of the United States, the antichrist would be unable to conquer the whole world. Therefore, the antichrist could skip all the trouble of conquering the United States and actually be an American. An invasion and conquest of the United States is virtually impossible. Where would his troops come from, France or Germany? The antichrist may very well skip the dramatics and get himself elected president of the United States. I know what you're saying, "Americans would never vote in the antichrist! The American voter is smart, well-informed, and sensible." I know it's hard to believe, but the American voter may just be duped in the future by such a man who promises the world to them.

Daniel explained that the antichrist would be of Roman descent. Roman descent could potentially be anyone of European descent today. Since seventy percent of Americans have European ancestry, it would be entirely possible. It is time to round up all the white people and send them back to Europe!

In the second decade of the 21st century, America is using its power for good around the globe. The benign giant provides stability economically and militarily. But imagine if one day the power and might of the United States is placed in the wrong hands, the hands of an antichrist? Overnight, the world's best military, technology, and economy would be firmly placed into the hands of the devil himself. Not a cheery thought.

By getting elected as the president of the United States of America, the antichrist would become the most powerful man in the world. In addition to the most powerful government position on earth, the antichrist would also have access to the best military machine in history, thus making his conquests of other kingdoms quite easy. I hope and pray the antichrist is not an American. Hopefully, America's future voters will have the sense not to elect the antichrist, but the man will masquerade as an "angel of light." The world's best deceiver will play his game on American citizens.

There are other scenarios. Perhaps America will hold out against the antichrist longer than others. Maybe the United States will be one of those nations continually undermining the antichrist's authority. It would be a shame to see such a great nation miss such an opportunity to be a thorn in Satan's side.

CONCLUSION: IS REVELATION BEING FULFILLED TODAY?

The world has shrunk from the days of the Roman Empire. The powers of Western Civilization have developed a global system that has paved the road for the feet of Daniel's statue to develop into the ten toes of global community. The United States protects this global system, acting as a stabilizer and enforcer.

Everything needed for a Western global dictatorship is present: military superiority, technology, communications, language, economic interdependence, global cooperation, and the presence of a single superpower protecting the system. Should the antichrist come from America, it would surely be easier. There is, however, hope that Americans would never willingly give up so much autonomy to such a dictator, let alone the antichrist.

Part II
FUTURE PROPHECIES AND CURRENT EVENTS

Chapter Three

GOG AND MAGOG: RUSSIA'S END-TIMES INVASION OF ISRAEL

The word of the lord came to me: "Son of man, set your face against Gog, of the land of Magog, the chief prince of Meshech and Tubal; prophesy against him and say: 'This is what the Sovereign Lord says: I am against you, O Gog, chief prince of Meshech and Tubal.' (Ezekiel 38:1–3)

For many years, distracted readers have glanced right past Ezekiel Chapters 38 and 39. In fact, most of Ezekiel is ignored by Christians and often dismissed as too hard to understand or just plain scary. Its frightening imagery makes timid readers search for nicer bedtime stories, such as baby Jesus in the manger. In fact, the first chapter usually scares readers off.

I looked, and I saw a windstorm coming out of the north – an immense cloud with flashing lightning and surrounded by brilliant light. The center of the fire looked like glowing metal, and in the fire was what looked like four living creatures... (Ezekiel 1:4–5a)

Okay, who put the script for the new *Aliens* movie in the Bible? If the timid reader works up the courage to see what Ezekiel is all about, he or she may continue to read about Israel's political and spiritual restoration (Ezekiel 37), the Gog/Magog invasion of Israel (Ezekiel 38, 39) and the rebuilding of the Millennial Temple (Ezekiel 40). Ezekiel Chapter 38 describes one of the great geopolitical predictions in the Bible.

The word of the lord came to me: "Son of man, set your face against Gog, of the land of Magog, the chief prince of Meshech and Tubal; prophesy against him and say: 'This is what the Sovereign Lord says: I am against you, O Gog, chief prince of Meshech and Tubal. I will turn you around, put hooks in your jaws and bring you out with your whole army—your horses, your horsemen fully armed, and a great horde with large and small shields, all of them brandishing their swords. Persia, Cush and Put will be with them, all with shields and helmets, also Gomer with all its troop, and Beth Togarmah from the far north with all its troops—the many nations with you.' (Ezekiel 38:1–6)

In one of the most straightforward prophecies in the Bible, God mentions actual nations that will do terrible things in the future. What exactly do these future nations have in mind?

In future years you will invade a land that has recovered from war, whose people were gathered from many nations to the mountains of Israel, which had long been desolate. They had been brought out from the nations, and now all of them live in safety. You and all your troops and the many nations with you will go up, advancing like a storm; you will be like a cloud covering the land. This is what the Sovereign LORD says: On that day thoughts will come into your mind and you will devise an evil scheme. You will say, "I will invade a land of unwalled villages; I will attack a peaceful and unsuspecting people—all of them living without walls and without gates and bars. I will plunder and loot and turn my hand against the resettled ruins and the people gathered from the nations, rich in livestock and goods, living at the center of the land." (Ezekiel 38:8–12)

The passage describes an invasion of an unsuspecting, secure Israel for the purposes of plunder. The attack occurs in "future years" or "latter days," common references to the end-times. The nations will assault the "mountains of Israel" (Ezekiel 38:8) for "plunder" (Ezekiel 38:12). It is important to note that God himself entices these nations down to their own destruction, a tribute to their depravity as nations.

Fortunately, the invasion is botched from the start, and God eventually destroys the invading army with literal fire from heaven. The entire world sees God's hand in the rescue of Israel, and many come to accept Christ as savior. This chapter will outline the basic turn of events in this prophecy, as well as the potential powers involved.

ISRAEL BACK IN THE HOLY LAND AFTER WORLD WAR II

The prophecies in Ezekiel could never take place without the existence of a Jewish state in Israel. The second regathering of Israel took place in 1948 after the calamity of the Holocaust and the brutal wars with Arab Palestinians. For the first time since the Romans exiled the Jews in the 1st century AD, there exists within the Holy Land an independent Jewish nation. In Matthew Chapter 24, Jesus himself describes this regathering.

> Now learn this lesson from the fig tree: As soon as its twigs get tender and its leaves come out, you know that summer is near. Even so, when you see all these things, you know that it is near, right at the door. Truly I tell you, this generation will certainly not pass away until all these things have happened. (Matthew 24:32–34)

Did Jesus want us to know the nutritional value of figs? Possibly, but the phrase "fig tree" was also a common reference in the Old Testament to the nation of Israel. The fig tree that bears fruit represented a spiritually revived Israel—one that has embraced Jesus as the Messiah. This has not happened nor will it until the Millennium. The fig tree in Matthew 24:32 only had tender twigs and leaves but no fruit. It is not yet spiritually alive. Israel is, however, very much alive politically (hence the leaves and twigs).

Jesus reiterated the Old Testament prophets' predictions that Israel would be regathered a second time. There is a similar prophecy in Ezekiel Chapter 37 regarding a valley of dry bones (politically restored Israel). Isaiah Chapter 11 also indicates that this second regathering was to take place in the future.

> In that day the Lord will reach out his hand a *second* time to reclaim the surviving remnant of his people from Assyria, from Lower Egypt, from Upper Egypt, from Cush, from Elam, from Babylonia, from Hamath and from the islands of the Mediterranean. (Isaiah 11:11)

Isaiah wrote these words down over 100 years before the first exile of Israel by the Babylonians in 583 BC. Isaiah's usage of the term "second time" is a clear indication that there are to be only two regatherings before the end comes. This is a powerful argument against those who say Israel can be exiled and regathered a hundred times before the Lord returns—not so according to Isaiah.[1]

Additionally, Jesus prophesied another end-times prediction in the very same chapter of Matthew. One of the signs of the end of the age, which precedes the regathering of Israel, was nation verses nation warfare.

> As Jesus was sitting on the Mount of Olives, the disciples came to him privately. "Tell us," they said, "when will this happen, and what will be the sign of your coming and of the end of the age?" Jesus answered: "Watch out that no one deceives you. For many will come in my name, claiming, 'I am the Christ,' and will deceive many. You will hear of wars and rumors of wars, but see to it that you are not alarmed. Such things must happen, but the end is still to come. Nation will rise against nation, and kingdom against kingdom. There will be famines and earthquakes in various places. All these are the beginning of birth pains." (Matthew 24:3–8)

Because this is a book primarily centered on the geopolitical components of prophecy, I will leave the earthquakes and false messiahs out of it for now, but Jesus uses a key phrase, "nation will rise against nation, and kingdom against kingdom." Most Dispensational Bible scholars agree that this is a reference to World War I and World War II.

Prior to this phrase, Jesus explains that there will be wars and rumors of war, but he specifically separates this phrase from the rest of the wars. Why? Two reasons: one, the world wars were unprecedented in size and scope. Second, according to Matthew 24:7-8, the world wars were to be the first sign that the end of the age had begun.[2] In the earlier verses of the chapter, Jesus explained the generic signs of the end of the age, including false messiahs and wars.[3] These happen all the time, but world wars have only happened twice, both within the past century.

Never before had so many nations and peoples gone to war against other nations and peoples. Even Uruguay got involved! In 1914, after years of intense rivalry amongst the Western powers, they tragically turned on each other with deadly precision.

Coined as the first modern wars, these were by far the deadliest conflicts the world had ever seen. At least thirty million people were killed in World War I. Twenty years later, the rise of Hitler's Nazi Germany and his allies in Italy and Japan led to an even greater slaughter. Some fifty million were killed in just six years. That's the equivalent of roughly one fifth of the US population. Jesus's predictions of worldwide warfare were to be taken as a sign of the end and a precursor to Israel's regathering in 1948.

WHAT THIS BATTLE IS NOT

Regarding Ezekiel's end-times prediction, this is not a battle for wimps. Ezekiel's prophecy represents a literal, end-times war involving a great number of nations. Neither has this battle ever taken place in history. God indicates that the battle will take place during the "latter days," a common reference to the end times. Ezekiel wrote this prophecy somewhere between 593-571 BC. Since that time, there has never been a battle ending with the fire of God's wrath upon the aggressors.

Other critics argue that the battle takes place during the Tribulation. This cannot be the case either. Both Daniel and Revelation explain that during the Tribulation, the antichrist (then leader of the western world) will make a peace agreement with Israel for seven years. In the middle of that peace agreement, the antichrist will break the pact and will seek to destroy all surviving Christians and Jews on the planet. During the first 3.5 years, Israel is living in relative peace and safety, protected by the Western world. During the last 3.5 years, Israel is in hiatus, being chased across the globe by the antichrist. There is no time or opportunity for a northern coalition to seek an invasion of Israel during the Tribulation.

Others may argue that this is the Gog/Magog battle referenced in Revelation Chapter 20. Again, the nature of this conflict is much different than Satan's last attack against Christ. First, God himself entices Gog down to Israel to be slaughtered. In Revelation Chapter 20, the devil is leading the forces for the sake of rebellion against God. Gog is clearly a man in Ezekiel, while Satan himself leads the forces in Revelation Chapter 20. Thirdly, the entire lost world joins Satan at the end of the Millennium, whereas only a coalition of nations is involved in Ezekiel's invasion of Israel.

This begs the question, "What the heck is this battle and when will it take place?" It is a future Middle Eastern conflict fabricated by a northern power for the purpose of plunder. No one knows for sure precisely when it will take place, but it will most likely happen before the Tribulation, and before or after the Rapture. (After the Rapture would be a fitting guess, given the lackluster response of the United States.)

God indicates that Israel will stand alone, and no nation will come to its aid. For as long as there are Christians in the United States, there will be an American desire to protect Israel. A Russian invasion of the Middle East would never be allowed while the Holy Spirit is still present in America.

THE POTENTIAL POWERS INVOLVED

It is important to keep in mind that Ezekiel is translating this vision with a 6th century BC outlook. Of course, he is not going to mention Russia or Turkey by name; but he is going to leave enough clues for modern-day readers to solve the puzzle. According to Ezekiel, the leader of this northern confederation happens to be Russia. Is anyone surprised?

RUSSIA: "GOG, MAGOG, MESHECH, AND TUBAL"

Ezekiel is quite clear as to who this future northern power will be.

Bible scholars agree that Gog is most likely a title for king or leader.[4] Needless to say, the new czar of Russia in all but name, Vladimir Putin, definitely fits the mold. The land of Magog is a reference to the ancient table of nations found in Genesis, referring to a broad Indo-European branch of peoples. In Ezekiel's day, the land of Magog was home to the Magogites.

The Magogites hailed from a region between Armenia and Persia in the Caucasus region.[5] As both the ancient Greek Herodotus, and the Jewish historian Josephus indicated, the Magogites were the ancestors of the powerful Scythians.[6] The Scythians in turn were a broad group of tribes and peoples who eventually settled in present-day Russia. According to Dr. Fausset, the Scythians at one point even tried to invade Egypt.[7]

During Ezekiel's time, Meshech and Tubal were both well-known tribes who, according to Assyrian writings, lived in northern Turkey.[8] These two tribes were eventually run off by more powerful tribes, but they migrated north, intermingling with the Magogites and Scythians north of the Black Sea in southern Russia.

As if particular names were not enough evidence, Ezekiel even describes where in relation to Israel this northern power was from—"a place from the far north" (Ezekiel 38:15). In ancient Hebrew writings, directions were always in relation to Israel's locale. Israel was the center of the world, so when Ezekiel wrote "far north," he meant the farthest remote northern locations (in relation to Israel). On a map, there is no doubt that Russia encompasses the far north of Israel.

It is no surprise that Russia will be the end times invader of Israel. From the pogroms of the 19th century to the Communist ideology of the 20th, Russia has been at odds with God and a persecutor of the Jewish people. The famous Soviet dictator Vladimir Lenin's last words were, "May God save Russia and kill the Jews."[9] Nice guy. Russia armed Israel's enemies during the Arab/Israeli wars, and even as late as 2006, armed Hezbollah with rockets and munitions.[10] Today, Russia continues to supply Israel's enemies, this time giving Iran access to nuclear technology.

IRAN: "PERSIA"

It doesn't get much easier than this one. Since ancient times, Persia had always been known as Persia, that is until the Germans convinced them they were special. The German quest for Aryan allies during WWII convinced Persia to change its name to Iran, which is Farsi for "Aryan."

Today, the Iranian leadership's desires are threefold: the destruction of the Jewish nation in Palestine, the acquiring of nuclear weapons, and the spread of Shiite Islam. Everyone has heard the fiery Iranian president denounce Israel while threatening nuclear attacks. It is quite easy to see Iran willingly join the northern coalition in an invasion of Israel.

ETHIOPIA, SUDAN, AND SOMALIA: "CUSH AND PUT"

Cush is a common reference to Ethiopia, one of the world's oldest civilizations, but it also encompasses nearby places such as Eritrea and Somalia. Put, often referred to as Libya, is not actually modern day Libya but rather a reference to the ancient land of Sudan, along with nearby nations along the Horn of Africa.

Ethiopia and Somalia aren't exactly super powers. In fact, they are two of the poorest nations on earth. They share a common history with nearby Islamic powers. This region of Africa also happens to be the most strategic of the continent, as it sits on the Gulf of Aden—the gateway to the Suez Canal. Becoming increasingly Islamic and desperate, it is no small stretch to see these nations join a future coalition for "plunder."

TURKEY: "GOMER AND ALL HIS BANDS"

Gomer presents more of a mystery as to its true identity. For a long time, Gomer was thought to be Germany, thanks to the Talmud's identification.[11] The mysterious mentioning of "all his bands" may be a reference to the reunification of Germany, both in 1870 and 1989. It is possible that Germany could be enticed to join an invasion of Israel. German Nazis nearly wiped out the Jews some seventy years ago, and the history of German anti-Semitism was strong throughout the Middle Ages. In addition, Germany's new energy ties with Russia may allow Russia to exert strong pressure on Germany, eventually forcing them to join the coalition.

The more likely candidate is Turkey. Gomer is an Assyrian reference to the ancient Cimmerians, a tribe who lived on the southern shores of the Black Sea in Asia Minor (Turkey).[12] Gomerites were also commonly referred to as Galatians.[13] Galatia, famously known as the location of one of Paul's churches, was a Roman province in Asia Minor. Moreover, the secular Muslim nation has become increasingly Islamic, leading to cooler relations with both Israel and the West.

TURKEY AGAIN, AND MAYBE ARMENIA: "BETH-TOGARMAH"

Beth-Togarmah was known to the ancient Roman historian Tacitus as Armenia,[14] while Josephus refers to Beth-Togarmah as the home of the Thrugrammeans, a derivation of Phrygians. The Phrygians were an ancient power located in central Turkey from 1200 BC to 600 BC, the same time period in which Ezekiel wrote his prophecy.[15] Beth-Togarmah could also be a loose reference to the Turkic-descended peoples of central Asia.[16] Either way, it seems that Armenians and Central Asian nations may be swallowed up with the great northern coalition. The "stan" nations of central Asia have long been dominated by the Russian and Turkic powers anyway.

Jerry Jenkins and Tim La Haye refer to this invasion in their famous *Left Behind* series as a botched air attack. More likely, these nations, along with an untold number of others, "the many nations with you," (Ezekiel 38:6) will strike deep into the mountains of northeastern Israel with a land invasion, only to be slaughtered.

MOTIVE

Why would anyone ever want to attack Israel? Obviously, Satan would like to see it fall, and he has a pretty strong grasp on the world at hand. Israel is the only country that Satan cannot add to his demonic realm (thanks to the archangel Michael who watches over Israel), and he rages against her with every lie imaginable. According to John Phillips, Satan has demons in every other nation's capital except Israel's, influencing leaders for evil rather than good.[17]

Satan's lies have permeated different societies' perceptions of the

Jewish people. In the Middle Ages, Jews were thought to have sacrificed Christian children. They were also blamed for poisoning well water during the Black Death. Hitler called them the inferior race. Spain killed and exiled thousands in their Inquisition, and today Iran threatens to annihilate them once again. Exiled, hunted, and exterminated, Jews have been treated as a pariah in most of the countries in which they have lived.

Today, there are over 130 million hostile Arabs surrounding only seven million Jews in Israel. Yet international anger over the plight of three million Palestinians seems to overshadow the violent rhetoric from Hamas and Hezbollah. Gaza-bound flotillas, supported by the Turkish government, seek to run the blockade summer after summer. Syrians stream across the northern border of the Golan Heights, sacrificing themselves in the name of "peace."

There is even a movement within the UN—strongly supported by some in the White House—to send a Peace Keeping force into Israel to protect the Palestinians from the Israeli "occupiers." In addition to satanic anti-Semitism, there also exists more tangible motivations for these countries to invade Israel: strategic, political, and financial plunder.

Strategically, Israel sits at the crossroads of three continents: Asia, Europe, and Africa. Since ancient times, superpowers have fought over this strategic strip of land, known as the Levant. No ancient power has been completely secure without controlling the Levant.[18] Today, Israel is more strategic than ever, sitting at the crossroads of the oil trade. Just miles from the Suez Canal and all the wealth of Arab oil, Israel is indeed a coveted land.

Politically, Israel is also the key to the Middle East. For an outside power who desires Middle Eastern dominance, what is the one country in the region that could be invaded without risking the wrath of two billion Muslims? Israel. Should Russia decide to invade Saudi Arabia, for instance, Iraq, Egypt, Syria, Yemen, Jordan, and even Turkey may turn against them.

Politically, Israel is crucial for solving the ancient Middle East peace dilemma. Every American administration from Truman to Obama has been obsessed with seeking a peace agreement between the Jews and the Palestinians. Just as the Philistines were a constant thorn in the side of ancient Israel, so too are the Palestinians today.

The assumption of American presidents has been that if there ever were a peace deal brokered between the two sides, anti-American hostility would cease. Arabs throughout the Middle East would look upon the US more favorably, possibly even embracing democracy for the first time in 4,000 years. Easing their access to oil would also be a plus. Instead of being called the Great Satan, the United States may be called the Great Negotiator. As the Bible indicated in Genesis, peace between these two sides will be impossible until the Millennium.

Today, President Obama is pressuring the Israeli government to renew peace talks with Hamas and Fatah, co-rulers of the Palestinian Authority. American/Israeli relations have never been worse. Obama has repeatedly declared his wishes for Israel to give the Palestinians all lands taken during the 1967 War, including the Gaza Strip, the West Bank, and half of Jerusalem. He also wishes the free flow of Palestinian exiles back into these lands.

Hmm, this is a tough call for Israeli policy-makers. Give away one third of Israeli land, allow two million Palestinian Arabs back into the country, and split the ancient Hebrew city of Jerusalem in half. Half of Jerusalem, ancient home to three of the world's most influential religions, would be given back to the Palestinian authority. Before 1967, no Christians or Jews were even allowed into the eastern half of Jerusalem. Regarding a land giveaway, Israel is already the size of New Jersey. Adherence to these new American demands would make Israel the size of Maryland.

The Gaza Strip and the West Bank are the Jewish spoils of war, prophesied in Isaiah 11:14. In the same chapter that Isaiah speaks of Israel's second regathering, he also predicts a future battle in which Israel gains more territories.

They will swoop down on the slopes of Philistia to the west; together they will plunder the people to the east. They will lay

hands on Edom and Moab, and the Ammonites will be subject
to them. (Isaiah 11:14)

Just after Israel had regathered a second time, war broke out in 1956
and then again in 1967. In the 1967 war, Israel captured the Gaza Strip
from the Egyptians and the Golan Heights from Jordan. Where exactly
are the "slopes of Philistia" today?" The Gaza strip! Who were the peoples
directly east of Israel? In antiquity the Ammonites, Edomites, and
Moabites lived on the other side of the Jordan River. Because these lands
were specifically regiven to the Israelites in prophecy, they will most likely
remain in Israeli hands until the Tribulation.

Despite the futility of the action, many world leaders will continue
to scheme over a peace deal in the Middle East, including the leader of
Russia. The peace talks could be his chance to "peacefully" invade the
Middle East—with UN approval. If successful, he would be seen as a
hero to many in the Muslim world by finally ending the Israeli "occupa-
tion." Iran and Turkey would insist on joining him for the purpose of
controlling Jerusalem. Each nation would be the regional leader for their
branch of Islam. Turkey would represent the Sunni Islamic world, while
Iran would represent the Shiites.

To top it off, the dissembling of one of the West's oldest allies would
be a slight against the Western powers. Every anti-American hooligan
on the planet could send troops to destroy Israel.

Financially, Israel is a regional bulwark of stability. As a representative
democracy, Israel gives its people and corporations the freedom to gain
wealth. Tourism and industry are also strong components of their economy. Israel has a stronger economy than all of its neighbors combined,
but there may be another potential source of revenue as well.

A recent Wall Street Journal article reads, "Could Israel become an
Energy Giant?" In recent years, scientists have uncovered a massive shale
deposit inside Israel. With technological innovations, this shale deposit
could produce up to 250 billion barrels of light crude oil.[19] Shale oil,
although difficult to extract, is still oil. Additionally, sixteen trillion cubic
feet of natural gas was discovered in 2010 off Israel's shores.[20] If utilized,

these findings could turn Israel into another Middle Eastern energy giant.

Despite the strategic, financial, or political reasons for invading Israel, the enemies of God are inevitably drawn for one reason or another to their ultimate destruction.

SITTING THIS ONE OUT: THE WESTERN WORLD AND THE ARAB WORLD

Sheba and Dedan and the merchants of Tarshish and all her villages will say to you, "Have you come to plunder? Have you gathered your hordes to loot, to carry off silver and gold, to take away livestock and goods and to seize much plunder?" (Ezekiel 38:13)

There will be two powerful blocs opposing, at least verbally, this invasion: the Western powers and the Arab world. "The Merchants of Tarshish and all her villages," (young lions in the KJV), is an Old Testament reference to the Western islands, or lands of the far west. In other passages, Tarshish was a reference to Western sea powers (Isaiah 60:9).[21] Tarshish was at other times a reference to Spain. Jonah tried to flee there after God ordered him to Nineveh. Tarshish was also interchangeably called Chittim, a common reference to the Roman lands to the west.

"The young lions" could have been a reference either to the number of Western countries or their colonies overseas in the New World. Altogether, the ships of Tarshish in Ezekiel's prophecy represent the end-times Western powers.

There are a number of reasons why the US and her western allies would oppose the invasion but not necessarily defend Israel. If the Rapture has already happened and the Christian lobby supporting Israel has disappeared, it is a foregone conclusion. It is also entirely possible that by this point, the United States will have abandoned her old ally Israel.

The rift has started with the Obama presidency, but who knows when or how it will end. Demands to cede lands to the Palestinians are not the most popular amongst Israeli Jews, and many Israelis feel that the President is openly siding with the Palestinians.

It is also evident that abandonment, or at least isolation of Israel has become strategically savvy to some pundits. No longer necessary to counter Soviet aspirations in the Middle East, Israel is no longer considered as strategically valuable to some policy makers. When the Communists were advancing upon Yemen, Egypt, and Syria, the Americans needed a stalwart democracy in the region to counter them. Many of the Jews who immigrated to Israel were from Western Europe, and shared the same cultural traits as America—particularly the concept of a democratic republic. The little democratic nation of Israel was a lone ally.

Screams from the Arab world of "down with the Great Satan and the Little Satan" have also taken their toll on American policy. Regardless of how loyal Israel has been to the United States over the past six decades, some American strategists prefer to throw them to the wolves. Isolating Israel may also help the US reach an accommodation with Iran.[22] In the minds of some American strategists, if a little separation from Israel eases Muslim rage, so be it.

Another less obvious reason for American and Western indifference is the energy relationship between Europe and Russia—Russia has it, Europe needs it. The Russians currently have a natural gas stranglehold on Germany and Eastern Europe. It could be that Europe, energy starved, may turn a blind eye to Russian expansion, thus pressuring the US to do the same.

Although the United States would hate to see the Russians destroy Israel, extenuating circumstances may cause them to hesitate. European or Muslim pressure may force America to sit back. Most likely the West may be stunned or completely surprised. The Russians were great at keeping secrets during the Cold War. Perhaps their agencies will keep a lid on this operation until it is too late for the Americans or Europeans to act. Phillips believes Ezekiel alludes to a Western counter attack as God "calls for a sword in all the mountains." (Ezekiel 38:21). This could be a generic reference to the wrath of God raining down on the coalition forces, or it may be a Western counter-attack against the northern coalition[23] after they recoup from the initial shock.

THE ARAB RESPONSE

The Arab response is mixed with both joy and dread. The reaction of Sheba and Dedan (Ezekiel 38:13) is that of outrage over the obvious goal of the mission—plunder. Sheba and Dedan are common references to Arab tribes living in the Arabian Peninsula. If the Russians come to plunder Israel, why stop there? Why not seize the entire oil region of the gulf? From Saudi Arabia to the Gulf States, wealthy oil sheiks would be terrified of a joint Russian/Turkish/Iranian invasion. They will condemn the invaders publicly, but would not have the power to stand up against them.

Saudi Arabia and the Gulf States have always been wealthy but never powerful, a volatile mix. They have relied on the United States to protect them, but when they see the US abandon Israel to the northern invaders, the Gulf Arabs will have no other choice but to bend the knee to the Russians.

On the other hand, some Arabs would respond with joy as their oldest enemy was finally being destroyed, and the Muslim Holy sites of Jerusalem would once again be in the hands of Muslims. Given the current state of the "Arab Spring," joy at Israel's demise is not a far stretch. From the streets of Gaza to Egypt's Tahrir Square, a multitude of young Muslim Arabs have taken their newfound freedom of speech as a license to spew hatred towards the nation of Israel. Many will indeed take the attack on Israel as a blessing.

Although a large number of Arabs resent the Jews, completely absent in this passage are three of Israel's oldest Arab foes: Egypt, Syria, and Iraq. From ancient times to the present, armies from these three regions have constantly attacked Israel. At first glance, it seems surprising that they would sit out on the final chance to attack Israel. These are not small, obscure nations, but are well known both today and in biblical times. Had they been involved, Ezekiel probably would have mentioned them.

As the Arab world's largest country, Egypt is often looked upon for leadership. Should Egypt join the invasion, many other Arab countries would follow. Despite the rage emanating from the Muslim Brotherhood and the newly elected Islamist President, Egypt is in no position to attack Israel. Besides, an absent or unstable Israel is bad for the Egyptian economy, as the two nations have grown increasingly interdependent within the last couple decades.

Iraq may possibly abstain from any fighting because it still has Western (American) troops or, at the very least, advisors stationed there. Although the president recently removed all combat troops from Iraq, there are still a great number of American civilians, contractors, and non-combat troops in the region. Iraq may also abstain because God has something else planned for that Arab nation. The ruins of Babylon will be rebuilt in the near future. Since the ruins are located just a few miles from Baghdad, the Iraqis are perfectly suited to do it.

Of the three, Syria would most likely join the invasion. Ezekiel explains that the invaders will use the mountains of Israel as an entryway into the country. The mountains of northern Israel lie very near the Golan Heights. Syria has wanted this region back ever since it was lost in the 1967 war. In order to use the Golan Heights as a way into Israel, the invaders would either have to conquer Syria, or coerce them into joining the attack; both are valid scenarios. With the current uprisings against the Assad regime, Syria's future is wide open.

Perhaps the greatest reason of all for the Arab absence from the invasion is the love and mercy of God. Having blessed the descendants of Abraham's son Ishmael and his subsequent descendants (as promised in Genesis), God would not want to see them destroyed in the coming invasion. The Lord promised Abraham that his descendants would be blessed, even the wild ones.

Conclusion of the Battle

The Russian-led invasion will not really be much of a battle. First, there will be an earthquake (Ezekiel 38:19), followed by potential attack from the West (38:21), which is then followed up by vicious infighting amongst the invaders themselves. Perhaps the Muslims will detest Russian drinking habits, or the Sunnis and Shiites will have a falling out as to who gets Jerusalem. The options for the invaders are endless, but in the end, they are finally destroyed by fire (Ezekiel 39:6). God even rains fire upon the "coastlands" and the land of Magog itself. If there are any Russians reading this book, it is time to buy a one-way ticket to the beaches of Florida.

Is the world setting itself up for the fulfillment of this prophecy sooner rather than later? Does Russia today have the will and means to carry out such an audacious attack? Are Russia, Turkey, and Iran aligning themselves together for the first time in history? We must now look at these individual nations under the microscope of geo-politics.

Chapter Four

IS ISRAEL SECURE TODAY?

You will say, "I will invade a land of unwalled villages; I will attack a peaceful and unsuspecting people—all of them living without walls and without gates and bars." (Ezekiel 38:11)

Every time I get a yearning to visit the Holy Land, I am discouraged by pessimists who say, "You have to be careful, it's dangerous over there. What if you get kidnapped, blown up, or shot?" Any number of those possibilities could happen to me here in a rough neighborhood around DC, perhaps even more so. Who knows, you may even get a paper cut reading this book, but that is the risk you take.

Every adult in Israel has to serve in the military for at least two years. This means that every Israeli knows how to handle a weapon. If they see a young man (or woman) nervously screaming "Allah Akbar," clutching a bomb detonator in his hand, they know exactly what to do.

The Israeli government uses every precaution to protect American tourists in the country. Its Intelligence Agency is one of the best in the world, and its military has proven itself quite capable of defending the tiny nation.

It seems hard to believe, but Israel is more secure today than they have been since the days of King Solomon. Despite the overwhelming hatred directed towards them, Israel is thriving. They dominate their neighbors economically and militarily. As stated by both Jesus and Isaiah, however, their spiritual awakening is yet to come.

Critics would claim Israeli security is nonsense; just look at Palestinian suicide bombers and terrorists. True, but experts agree that the Palestinians could never destroy the country. They lack the military capabilities and organization. Ezekiel claims that during the Gog/Magog invasion, Israel is:

a land that has recovered from war, whose people were gathered from many nations to the mountains of Israel, which had long been desolate. They had been brought out from the nations, and now all of them live in safety. (Ezekiel 38:8)

Has the relative safety prophecy been fulfilled today? Jews returned to Israel in 1948 after the worst war the world had ever seen. They came from Poland, Germany, Russia, and even more distant places, such as Iran and Ethiopia. When they arrived in Palestine, it was nothing more than a desolate wasteland. The local Arab population was small and dispersed amongst Jerusalem and a few villages. Since 1948, the Jews have revived the land agriculturally and economically. Yes, this part of the prophecy has indeed been fulfilled.

The text in Ezekiel does not say that Israel is living in peace today. The word "security" means confidence but not necessarily peace.[1] To be sure of Israel's safety, two relationships must be examined: Israel's relations with its neighbors and its relations with more distant superpowers. As George Friedman points out, when Israel is the strongest among its neighbors, there is little to fear. Egypt, Lebanon, Jordan, and Syria all have grievances with Israel, yet none can do anything about it.

Although Egypt's Muslim Brotherhood has recently been ratcheting up the war rhetoric, it is neither prudent nor logistical for them to attack Israel. Egypt had help in 1956, 1967, and 1973 against Israel, primarily with weapons from the Soviet Union but also with troops from Iraq, Algeria, Libya, Saudi Arabia, Jordan, Lebanon, and Syria. Should Egypt wish to attack Israel today, they may do so largely alone (unless Russia gets involved).

Logistically, it is nearly impossible for Egypt to attack on its own through the Sinai Peninsula.[2] A series of deserts, mountains, and wastelands presents a difficult challenge for supply lines. Egyptian supply lines would be easy targets for the Israeli air force.

Economically, the two countries have become quite interdependent. Egypt relies on Israel for much of its technology and industrial products, whereas Israel relies on Egypt for energy. Despite radicals damaging the pipeline between the two countries in recent months, Egypt would not be wise to damage the relationship.

Of all Israel's neighbors, the Hashemite kingdom of Jordan has the best relationship with Israel. Jordan, unlike most Arab nations, lacks oil-fields. Being landlocked also makes Jordan dependent upon Israel for trade. During the Arab-Israeli wars, Jordan followed along with stronger Arab nations. Today, the King of Jordan realizes that Jordan's safety depends upon Israel's safety. Jordan lacks the strength or motivation to ever launch another attack on Israel.

Lebanon poses somewhat of a threat simply due to its location. The coastal plain that reaches from northern Lebanon down the coast of Israel into Gaza is a flat and fertile region.[3] Should a distant power seek to invade Israel, they may choose Lebanon as a landing dock. In 2006, Hezbollah fighters used Lebanon as a supply depot and defensive position as they launched thousands of rockets into Israel. The Lebanese government could do little to stop the Israeli army from invading Lebanon to deal with Hezbollah, but this chink in Israel's army has not been forgotten.

Lebanon is too embroiled in political infighting between its Christian and Muslim populations to be much of a threat. Lebanese officials are usually more wary of Syria than of Israel.

The Syrians present the largest threat to Israel. On their own, the Syrians lack the ability to defeat Israel, but when concerted with larger powers, they can be a menace. Historically, Israel has only been vulnerable from the Northeastern passes of the Golan Heights, situated between the mountains and the Sea of Galilee.[4] The Sinai and Arabian Deserts protect Israel to the South and East, and the Mediterranean Sea shelters Israel from the West. Babylonian and Assyrian armies crossed through the northeastern pass in ancient times, and Gog and his horde will try to exploit the pass in the future.

Of the Arab nations, the Syrians have the best relationship with both Iran and Russia. The current embattled dictator of Syria, Bashar al-Assad, has close ties to Moscow and Tehran. Even if he were ousted in the current Syrian uprisings, the more Islamic-minded factions of Syria could easily be persuaded to allow the vast armies to pass through their territory. In other words, Syria will most likely help no matter who is in charge.

Although Israel is isolated, their neighbors pose a minimal threat today, something that could not have been said forty years ago. Besides, the Syrian government distrusts the Egyptians almost as much as it distrusts the Israelis. The real threats, as always, come from distant powers.

Babylonians, Assyrians, Greeks, and Romans were all distant superpowers. Israel was never annihilated and exiled by neighbors like the Philistines or Moabites. Should a northern power such as Russia, or even regional powers like Iran and Turkey, seek to destroy Israel, it could be quite possible but for two snags: God won't let them, and the United States is his instrument of protection (for the moment).

Israel's Relations with Superpowers

To put it lightly, the Jews have had a rough existence on this planet. Getting destroyed once is more than enough pain, let alone twice as the Jews were—three times when one counts the Holocaust. By the time of their second exile in the 1st century AD, the Jews had already been dealt a calamitous history with world powers, a theme that seems to continue with the Jews even to this day.

Their first ordeal with a superpower left them enslaved for 400 years by the ancient pharaohs of Egypt. The Assyrian superpower was no better, having conquered and enslaved the northern tribes of Israel in 722 BC. The Babylonians one-upped the Assyrians by destroying Jerusalem and its Temple and enslaving the rest of the southern tribes of Judah in 583 BC. Life for the Jews fared better after the Persians swept the Middle East, given that they were allowed to return to Israel in 538 BC to start over. This was the first regathering, foretold by Old Testament prophets.

The peace did not last long. A Macedonian king brought war back to the Middle East in his smashing victories over the Persians in the 4th century BC. Alexander the Great did little harm to the Jews. They paid their taxes, submitted to his authority, and did not nag him about his partying habits. When he died without an heir in 332 BC, Israel once again became a battleground between two new regional powers—two Greek successor states: the Seleucid dynasty of Syria and the Ptolemaic pharaohs of Egypt.

The protracted 200-year struggle between Egypt and Syria was predicted by Daniel in Chapter 11, 400 years before the events ever happened. Unfortunately, the struggle ended with a pig being sacrificed in the Jewish temple by a nihilistic king known as Antiochus Epiphanes (who proclaimed himself a god). The Jews finally managed to kick the Greeks out only to be reconquered by the largest superpower of all— Rome.

The Roman period was not entirely negative. It was during the 1st century that Jesus came to earth, bringing salvation to all who believe in his message of redemption and forgiveness of sin. After the resurrection, the Christian church spread rapidly despite persecution. The nation of Israel, on the other hand, was in trouble both politically and spiritually. For one, a majority of the Jewish people rejected Christ as the Messiah, missing out on the greatest gift in history.

Secondly, a combination of inept Roman governors and fiery Jewish zealots led to three Jewish revolts, culminating in the destruction of Jerusalem in 70 AD. It was the very destruction prophesied by Jesus himself in Matthew Chapter 24.

The Jews were then scattered across the globe a second time. Persecution, a constant trouble for the Jews, plagued them until it reached an all time high in 20th century Europe. In the early phases of WWII, Hitler put into effect his plan to "move evolution along more quickly" by extinguishing inferior races. Commonly referred to as the "Final Solution," the Holocaust took the lives of six million Jews, nearly two thirds of the European Jewish population.

Despite Israel's terrible history with superpowers, they would, from time to time, play the larger powers off one another. Whenever this tactic did not work, they sought the protection of one superpower. In ancient times, this approach got Israelite kings in trouble. Rather than seeking the Lord for protection, the Israelite leaders went to the Babylonian and Egyptian kings, which ultimately led to the Israelite's exile and destruction.

The first superpower protector of Israel was ancient Persia under Cyrus the Great. Later, Queen Esther was able to protect the Jews, using her influence with King Xerxes. In recent history, the British were the reluctant protectors of Israel until 1948, allowing the Jews safe passage to Palestine for resettlement. France, and ironically, the Soviet Union sought to protect them in the early 1950s. Today their super-protector is the United States.

American-Israeli Relationship

Contrary to popular belief, the Americans first sought the affections of the Arabs, not the Israelis. After Arab-American relations went sour in 1956, Egypt led most of the Arab nations into the Soviet tent. It was then that Israel and the United States found themselves allied together against the Soviets and most of the Arabs.[5]

A number of American presidents were huge supporters of Israel. Truman and Eisenhower stuck by Israel even when it was strategically unpopular to do so. Truman knew the Biblical prophecies about Israel, and he decided to treat them with kindness. Kennedy saw them as a valued partner in the Cold War. When Kennedy was suddenly assassinated and Lyndon Johnson took office, he told an Israeli diplomat, "You have lost a great friend, but you have gained a better one."[6]

Johnson, a southern Baptist, believed deeply in the Bible's prophecy that God would "bless those who bless thee and curse those who curse thee," regarding the Jewish people. His support for the Israelis during the 1967 war was instrumental to their success.[7] From Truman to George W. Bush, most American presidents have felt an obligation to protect Israel. This pattern has changed under the presidency of Barack Obama. With the changing temperature of relations has come a fear in the minds of both Jews in Israel and Christians in the United States—will the US still protect Israel?

From UN plans to partition Israel into two nations to President Obama's repeated demands that Israel withdraw from Gaza and the West Bank, it seems that Israel is losing its superpower protection. In addition to the recent American demands that Israel return to the pre-1967 borders, the president has been quick to condemn Israel.

In the summer of 2010, a flotilla carrying aid, but also violent peace activists (ironic isn't it?) posing as aid helpers, made its way to the shores of Gaza. The Israeli navy ordered the ship to halt. When that order was ignored, Israeli commandos boarded the ship, where they were assaulted by dozens of "peace activists" with metal rods and even knives. In the end, nine activists lost their lives and Israel was in the crosshairs of every media organization in the world. As if that were not enough, the White House condemned the Israelis rather than the "peace activists" and supported any UN inquiries into the incident.

The changing relationship between Israel and the United States is alarming but should not be surprising. In past decades, Israel needed American support to help defend herself against her immediate Arab neighbors. The United States, in turn, needed Israel as a strategic ally against communism.

Unfortunately, some American policy makers now see their relationship with Israel as more of a liability than an asset. In today's world, the threat of communism has been replaced by the threat of terrorism. The theory, albeit flawed, is that Muslim extremism, driven by anger at the Jewish state, spills over against America for supporting Israel. The idea? Stop supporting those mean Israelis and those nice terrorists will leave America alone.

As depressing as this may be, Ezekiel's prophecies indicate this relationship will continue to devolve. In order to appease Muslim allies, the US may continue to distance itself from Israel. For whatever reason, America may not stand up against an invasion of Israel by a coalition of larger nations.

ISRAEL TODAY

Despite the souring relations with the USA, Israel is as safe as they will ever be this side of the Millennium. During the Cold War, nearby Arab nations threatened the very existence of the Jewish state with their repeated invasions. Yet even with Soviet support, Israel's neighbors failed to destroy Israel. Now, Israel's military capacity is even greater while its neighbors remain divided and politically unhinged.

Dominant militarily and economically, Israel can fend off most invaders. The exception to this rule is the persistence of a distant super-power, or a joint coalition of larger nations like Russia, Iran, and Turkey. An indication of how soon this invasion may take place is seen in Ezekiel 38:8, "You will invade a land that has recovered from war…" That was almost seventy years ago. If Russia is ever going to invade Israel, they must do it soon.

Chapter Five

WILL RUSSIA SOON INVADE THE MIDDLE EAST?

In future years you will invade a land that has recovered from war, whose people were gathered from many nations to the mountains of Israel, which had long been desolate. They had been brought out from the nations, and now all of them live in safety. (Ezekiel 38:8)

I f I had stated twenty years ago, just after the fall of the Soviet Union, that Russia would once again be powerful enough to invade the Middle East, I would have been laughed right out of elementary school. Seriously, I was only nine. No one could have predicted Russia's quick rise over the past two decades, except perhaps those who knew the prophecies of Ezekiel.

Son of man, set your face against Gog, of the land of Magog, the chief prince of Meshech and Tubal; prophesy against him and say: This is what the Sovereign Lord says: I am against you, O Gog, chief prince of Meshech and Tubal. (Ezekiel 38:1–2)

In future years you will invade a land that has recovered from war, whose people were gathered from many nations to the mountains of Israel, which had long been desolate. They had been brought out from the nations, and now all of them live in safety. (Ezekiel 38:8)

Could Russia today fulfill this prophecy? Despite their relative poverty and frigid climate, Russia has always been a powerful nation and brutal to match. Just as an abused child may one day grow into an abusive adult, so too did Russia come of age in an abusive environment. Ruled by the oppressive Mongols for three centuries, the Russian people were used to violence. The Mongols were finally defeated by the Russian prince Ivan the Terrible in 1533. Ivan, the first czar and founder of modern Russia, was nicknamed "Terrible." As history indicates, he was a paranoid psycho who killed a lot of his people, including his own son.

Medieval Russia was a rough neighborhood. One of Europe's worst institutions, serfdom, was abandoned by most of Western Europe during the 12th and 13th centuries but remained strong in Russia until the 1860s. Serfs were not only bound to the land, but they were also bound to their masters, quite different from the life of a western medieval peasant. The majority of Russians were enslaved to the Tsar and his ruling class throughout most of Russia's history.

Russians also had terrible tempers when it came to visitors and immigrants. The "pogroms," or purges of the 19th century, left thousands of Jews and Gypsies murdered in the streets just for fun.

When the Great War broke out, the Russians were incredibly outmatched by the efficient German forces. Germans attacked Russian positions with tanks, mustard gas, and planes, while Russians countered with cavalry on horseback and aging rifles. Most Russians were lucky even to be armed with a rifle.

The Russian people were used to brutal oppression and abject poverty, but they were not used to dying so quickly in a war very few people understood. The tide turned against Tsar Nicholas II and his family. A terrible economy, a losing battle against the Germans, and a rising menace known as Communism finally forced the Tsar to abdicate the throne.

The Russian revolution of 1916 promised the people hope and change, and change they got. Instead of various degrees of poverty, the entire country became poorer with the advent of Bolshevik communism. Under the guise of equality, the masses were then enslaved to the party rulers.

In addition to murdering Tsar Nicholas II and his family in the basement of a country home, the Bolshevik Communists instigated many of history's most tragic institutions. The concept of collective farming, which led to the starvation of millions, was one such institution. The USSR was also the first country to establish atheism as the official religion. Millions of Christians, Jews, Muslims, and Buddhists were persecuted during the Communist era.

Russia had become a police state, encouraging its people to spy on each other. Even families were exploited into spying inside their own homes. Millions of Russians disappeared under the rule of Joseph Stalin, perhaps the cruelest dictator in history. Stalin had members of his own family murdered.

Despite having overwhelming numbers, the Russian armies in WWII initially caved to the sleek, German war machine. Why? Upon Stalin's ascension to the communist throne, he systematically killed most of his generals for fear they might overthrow him. Lucky dissidents found themselves in the Siberian gulag work camps. Stalin was not the greatest tactician. Despite his violent, paranoid demeanor, Stalin eventually overpowered the Nazi forces with sheer numbers of soldiers.

What followed was a period of suspicion and fear known as the Cold War. Soviet and American spy agencies waged a silent war against one another. Eventually, Russia collapsed under its own ideology, as communism suppressed innovation or investment. Private individuals kept little of their earnings and lost incentive to invest or explore. The Russians simply ran out of money to pay for all of their weapons' programs. What followed was the disintegration of the Soviet Union and the arrival of the ex-communist nations on to the global market.

RUSSIA'S COMEBACK

It should come as no surprise today that Russia is once again becoming a regional power. Geographically, Russia is a giant. The arctic tundra of Siberia and the mountains of Asia protect its eastern flank from Chinese or Japanese threat. Deserts protect its underbelly, while the vast steppes of Eastern Europe present a logistical challenge for any Western invader. Following in the footsteps of Napoleon's failed 1812 Russian invasion, Hitler too forgot the frigid cold of Russian winters, as well as the sheer size of the country.

Russia has also come into a wealthy energy inheritance. After the fall of communism, Russian corporations were finally allowed to tap into the vast mineral wealth of Russia. Russia is currently the number one exporter in the world of natural gas and the number two exporter of oil, behind only Saudi Arabia. If Russia hadn't sold Alaska to the United States, imagine how much more oil and natural gas they would have accumulated.

Upon his appointment as President of the Russian federation, Vladimir Putin spent the next few years nationalizing the country's energy companies, including Gazprom, the leading energy company of Russia.[1] Since that time, the Russian government has used energy as both a bargaining chip and a strategic weapon.

Countries around the region rely almost solely on Russian energy. Turkey receives eighty percent of its energy from the Russian's blue stream gas pipeline,[2] while eighty percent of Ukraine's energy costs come from Russia as well.[3] In 2003, Germany struck an energy deal with Russia, allowing an oil pipeline known as the Nord Stream to flow directly from Russia, bypassing Poland, and straight into Germany.[4] As if Germany were not dependent enough upon Russia for energy, this deal effectively makes Russia Germany's number one supplier of energy.

Today, Russian pipelines web across nearly all of Europe. According to a recent article from *The Guardian*, up to fifty percent of Europe's natural gas will be controlled by Russia by 2030.[5] Should Russia threaten to cut off the supplies, it could be devastating for Europeans. According to European strategist Marc Huybrechts, once Russia's democracy experiment failed, it allowed the central government to seize the energy industry in order to enlarge its power.[6] Despite failing to become a democracy, Russia's energy has allowed it to become a power player once again.

Russia's president, Dmitri Medvedev, is simply a puppet holding the seat of power until Putin is ready to become president once again in 2012. Regarding his "reelection" in 2012, Putin had a plan to keep the military in his corner during the election. First, soldiers would be awakened with "pleasant music" to remind them who really cared for their well-being—Putin and the United Russia Party.[7] This would be followed by a free breakfast and encouraging words to go vote for Vlad![8]

Prime Minister Putin is no friend of democracy. While he was busy seizing private property for the state, his minions were also engaged in confiscating most of the country's media outlets.[9] Political opponents have been exiled, bullied, or silenced. An ex-spy himself, Putin has continued to use one of the world's best spy agencies not only to spy on his enemies but also on his own people.

Like their vodka and their spies, the Russian people also seem to enjoy the strong hand of a dictator. In 2006, fifty-eight percent of Russians polled wanted Putin for a third straight term. When this same poll asked Russians if they would vote for Stalin if he were still alive, twenty-four percent said yes.[10] Regarding the collapse of the Soviet Union, Putin said it was, "the greatest geopolitical catastrophe of the century."[11] Really, Vlad?

Russia has increasingly been a thorn in America's side, opposing nearly every American operation from the war in Iraq to sanctions on Iran. The Russians are no friends of America. Despite the 2010 "reset" with Russian relations, Russo-American relations have reached cold war levels.

American diplomats serving in Russia and ex-satellite nations today complain of Russian intimidation and "dirty tactics."[12] American diplomats receive threatening anonymous phone calls, returning home to find their apartments broken into and ransacked but with nothing taken. They even find cigarette butts on their kitchen tables and feces on the walls of their bathrooms. American diplomats file complaints against these gross invasions of privacy but to no avail.[13]

Russia has even sought to intimidate America's eastern European allies, evidenced in the 2008 invasion of Georgia and the browbeating of Poland over missile deployment. Before the invasion, Georgia wanted to become part of NATO. The Russians may have invaded Georgia just to show America that Georgia belonged in the Russian sphere. The invasion may have simply been a "stay out" warning.[14] Poland is scared to death of Russia, yet America cannot even give them strategic defense missiles without Russia's screaming about their national security. Rumors of another cold war with Russia are no longer rumors; the second cold war has already begun.

For all its bluster, this second cold war will be short. According to demographics, Russia is a short-term power. Many geopolitical pundits agree that Russia has serious issues if it wants to gain long-term power. Demographics create the most serious problem for the Russians.

Russia is running out of Russians. It has the fastest population decline in the world. Between 2010 and 2025, Russia will experience a full ten percent decline in their population, or roughly a drop from 147 million to 133 million.[15] By 2050, Russia will have seen a drop of nearly twenty-five percent of their current population.[16] Friedman predicts Russia will collapse much earlier than 2050, perhaps in the mid 2020s.[17]

Why is Russia's population dropping at such a dramatic rate? Low birth rates and high death rates would be the simple answer. For one, Russian men aren't known for aging well, due to both the high abuse of alcohol and to hard lives. Secondly, after the fall of Communism, many Russian women desired not to raise families but rather to go out into the new world of capitalism and make some money. Like many Western nations, the rise of women in the workplace has led to a necessary drop in birthrates.

Thirdly, Russia has one of the highest abortion rates in the world. A whopping seventy percent of all Russian pregnancies were terminated in 2004.[18] The lack of proper contraceptives, coupled with the apparent disregard for human life, has crippled Russia, perhaps permanently.

The demise of Russia's population hangs over Putin's head like an anvil. He has even offered to pay families to have more Russian babies. The world may see Russia acting much quicker than normal to subvert their demographic crisis. Nevertheless, if they wait too long, there will be no Russians to field their armies. To combat this dire situation, Putin's actions have shown glimpses of his geostrategic plan for the future.

RUSSIA'S SEVEN-STEP PLAN FOR WORLD DOMINATION:

1. FIND MORE RUSSIANS

If you can't breed them, find them. Russia has a high number of expatriates living in nearby lands. Ukraine has the largest number of Russians, with the Crimea's population being eighty percent Russian.[19] Perhaps the best case of Russian "baby stealing" can be seen in their recent invasion of Georgia. South Ossetia, a northern province of Georgia, holds a large number of Russians. When this region broke away from Georgia, Russia took its chance to bring them back into the fold.

The nearby neighbor of Belarus is ethnically Russian as well. They are all but begging to be reunited with their big Slavic brother. In fact, there is a Pan-Slavic Union plan floating around Eastern Europe today. The Pan-Slavic Union would see Ukraine, Belarus, and potentially the Slavic Balkans united under one rule.[20]

The ex-Soviet Central Asian nations have a lower number of Russians, but do not be surprised to see these countries quickly brought once again into the power sphere of the old Russian Tsars. Operation "find-more-Russians" is well underway.

2.   RECLAIM THE OLD SOVIET SPHERE OF POWER AND EXPAND THE BORDERS

Part of the power of Soviet Russia lay in its strategic size and depth. When Russia occupied the Baltic States, along with Ukraine and Belarus, they held excellent strategic depth, but now Moscow lies only a few hundred miles away from the border. Reclaiming Ukraine and Belarus are a must for Russia's security in the future.[21] Napoleon and Hitler both learned that Russia's strategic depth makes her nearly impregnable, yet Russians will not forget the damage inflicted by these Western powers.

Additionally, Russia will want to expand its southern and eastern borders by readmitting, or at least gaining power over the "stans" (Kazakhstan, Turkmenistan, Uzbekistan, Kyrgyzstan, and Tajikistan) of central Asia. Central Asia has historically partnered with either Russia or Turkey, and sometimes both. Additionally, these nations are so dependent upon Russia for trade and energy that they will have little choice but to give into Russian demands.

Putin has voiced his approval for a Eurasian Union similar to the European Union, only focused around Russia.[22] If his plans succeed, Putin will have rebuilt the old Tsarist Russian Empire in a matter of years.

Russian activity in the Caucasus region has also shown glimpses of this strategy. Armenia has strong ties with Russia, as does the minority Russian population in Georgia. Azerbaijan is more closely associated with Iran and Turkey but, nonetheless, would have little choice should Russia seek to have its way with the small countries.

3. FIND MORE WARM-WATER SEAPORTS

Russia is cold. Its water is colder. Accessible waterways cannot be frozen solid half of the year. Russia has always been on the lookout for warmer ports. This desire has led to wars with Turkey, Japan, and even Sweden. Who remembers Sweden ever fighting with anyone? The Baltic States may have a target on their backs because of their position on the Baltic Sea. Additionally, Israel would make a great warm-water port, would it not?

4. MAKE MORE FRIENDS IN THE MIDDLE EAST

Russia can be quite amiable when it suits her. Russia has always had an eye for friends in the Middle East. Even before the oil days, Russia lusted after the warm water ports and strategic locale of Middle Eastern lands. Today, Russia holds one significant advantage over the West regarding the Middle East; simply put, Russia is not part of the West. During the 19th century race for colonies, Russia sat out of the game, allowing Western European nations to carve up the Middle East.[23] Arab hostility towards this era of history can still be heard with cries of "imperialism," or "colonizers" directed towards Britain, France and even the US.

During the Cold War days, Russia was busy arming Arab regimes and promoting socialism. Algeria, Iraq, Syria, Libya, Yemen, and the Palestinians all received aid from the Soviets during the 1980s.[24] The USSR also had a military alliance with Nasser and the Egyptians during the 1950s and 1960s. After the Soviet era, Russia increased its activities in the Middle East, particularly with Turkey and Iran.

Historically, Turkey and Russia have been the worst of enemies. From 1677 to 1918, these two nations fought on thirteen different occasions.[25] As a member of NATO, Turkey remained an enemy of Russia until the collapse of the USSR in 1991. Russians and Turks fought over the Black Sea, the Crimean Peninsula, the Balkan Peninsula, and even over women. Back in the 16th and 17th centuries, the Ottoman Turks used to buy female Russian slaves from Tatar slave-traders, for they were quite valued for their shocking blonde hair.

In the 21st century, however, their relationship has thawed considerably. Russia is Turkey's number one trading partner, as well as Turkey's number one supplier of energy.[26] In return, Turkey is Russia's number one supplier of low-cost imports.[27] The 2008 Russian invasion of Georgia illustrates how close the two nations have become. Turkey's President Erdogan was one of the few leaders to come out in defense of Russia's aggression.

Many in the West feel uncomfortable with the growing closeness of Turkey and Russia. In 2008, the countries agreed to have yearly joint naval operations in the Black Sea, known as "BlackSeaFor."[28] From natural gas to nuclear energy tips, Russia and Turkey have benefited greatly from their mutual relationship. Putin was even the first Russian leader to ever visit Turkey.[29] Turkey also happens to be the number one tourist destination for Russians. During the frigid Russian months of October through May, there are thousands of Russian tourists sunning on the warm Mediterranean beaches of Turkey.

Perhaps the only other Middle Eastern country to garner so much adoration from Russia is Iran. For one, they have so much in common. Russia, Iran, and Turkey all share bitterness towards the Western powers, especially the United States. Ever wonder why Russia is constantly protecting and enabling Iran? Perhaps it empathizes with the Islamic Republic of Iran, but more than likely they all share a hatred for Israel. Russia does the best at masking this hatred, but it comes out from time to time.

Even in the pre-Putin days, Russia sold four billion dollars worth of weapons to Iran from 1992-2000.[30] Since 2000, the Russian government has assisted Iranians with air-defense systems, training, as well as a nuclear energy program.[31] The cheery relationship between Russia and Iran has not always been so cheery.

Russia occupied Iran during WWI to keep the Turks out and again in WWII to keep the Nazi's out. The Russian invasion of Afghanistan in the 1970s did nothing to warm relations. It was only during the Iran-Iraq War that Russia and Iran realized they had a common enemy—the USA. The Soviets saw a chance to destroy one of America's allies in the region (Iraq) by throwing money and weapons to the Iranians. The supply of weapons has continued since.

Another comfy relationship between Russia and a Middle Eastern nation is that with Syria. As stated previously, the Syrian regime is propped up primarily by Iran but also by Russia. Even as Assad has reportedly killed thousands of his own people, the Russians have refused to go along with a UN resolution to put an end to the violence. While most countries have respected the sanctions placed against Syria, the Russians have continued to sell weapons to Assad.

In fact, the Russians have decided to go one step further in their protection of the Syrian dictator. In March of 2012, the Russian troops first entered Syria. Known as "anti-terror" special forces, the Russians have landed a number of troops onto Syrian shores.[32] Their mission is murky, and the Russians have been hush-hush over the actual number of troops they have landed, but it goes to show how important the Assad regime has become for Russia.

5. CREATE A RUSSIAN ENERGY MONOPOLY

By making Eastern Europe and Germany dependent upon Russian energy, the Kremlin has developed a taste for energy power. They have already used this power to squeeze Ukraine into concessions, and Germany is hesitant to upset Russia for this very reason. Increasingly, Russia has made calls for an Eastern Energy Bloc. Not necessarily a monopoly, the bloc would be more of a cartel.

So far, Russia has made concerted efforts to set up a Eurasian energy bloc similar to OPEC with Iran, China, and Turkey.[33] Creating an alternative OPEC cartel with Russia at the helm would give Putin and the Kremlin incredible bargaining power over oil prices. Fortunately for Europe and the rest of the world, these nations have had other, more pressing matters to attend.

6. CREATE A UNIFIED COALITION AGAINST THE UNITED STATES

It is one thing to oppose the United States alone, but when there are a dozen nations aligned against the US, it's another matter entirely. Much like schoolyard bullies will join together to terrorize the neighborhood children, Russia will seek like-minded friends. In fact, most of America's future policy will be spent seeking to isolate Russia in her quest for allies.

Russia will continue to circumvent America's power across the Eurasian region. Should Russia seek to pressure and bully its neighbors, it could bring a sizable amount of the globe against America. As stated earlier, it is possible that Germany and Eastern Europe would be silenced into neutrality or even forced into a reluctant role, due to their Russian energy addiction. The old Soviet satellite nations such as Belarus and Ukraine, as well as Central Asia, Turkey, Iran, possibly China, and most likely Cuba and Venezuela would join any America-bashing party. I'm sure Sean Penn will be there as well.

7. SEIZE ISRAEL

Russia's last grasp for global domination will be a land grab of Israel herself. Russia has been moving the chess pieces steadily towards this direction for some time. Acquisition of Israel would solve nearly all of Russia's problems. In fact, Russia may have thought about it once before.

In 1982, during the height of the Israeli-Lebanese War, Israeli forces captured a massive Soviet arms cache. "The Underground tunnels in Lebanon stored enough Soviet arms to invade the entire Middle East," Prime Minister Begin proclaimed after having seen the cache.[34] There were more arms than any Lebanese military force could ever use, and the Israelis sincerely believed Russia was heading their way soon. Should Russia decide to strengthen their "anti-terror" troops now placed in Syria, they would be in an even better position to invade Israel than they were in 1982.

An invasion of Israel would place Russia at the strategic center of the world, just miles from oil in every direction, thereby giving Russia a chance to expand its energy monopoly and borders. It would also be a tremendous slap in the face to the Western powers, as well as acquiring a nice set of warm water ports.

Russia's scramble for world domination is well on its way. If they want to have a functioning economy and a sizeable army, however, they must act quickly.

Chapter Six

TURKEY ANYONE?

Also Gomer with all its troops, and Beth Togarmah from the far north with all its troops—the many nations with you. (Ezekiel 38:6)

I t was time for the Ottoman Empire to make a decision. It was October of 1914, nearly four months into the Great War, and the Ottomans still hadn't chosen a side. Feeling pressure from both the Germans and the British, the Ottomans were torn. The British had helped the Ottomans manage and keep Egypt under control, while the Germans had become a valued trading partner to the Empire.

It was in October that the Ottomans made the fateful decision that would lead to the collapse of one of history's longest running Muslim empires. The Ottomans decided to back the Kaiser and his modernized German army. It was the obvious choice, for the German army was the best in Europe by far.

The Great War went poorly for the Ottomans. Despite holding off the British at Gallipoli, Ottoman forces were outmatched. The British captured Palestine and managed to sway a majority of the Arabs against their Ottoman masters. The famous Lawrence of Arabia struck a terrible blow to the Ottomans, convincing local Arab sheiks to attack the Turkish positions at Aqaba. Finally, the Ottomans lost the climactic battle on the Plain of Megiddo, losing the majority of their Middle Eastern lands to the British.

In 1918, the lands of the old Ottoman Empire had been sliced, parceled, and given to the allied powers in nice, neat packages with bows on top. Great Britain nabbed Egypt, Palestine, and parts of Iraq, while France grabbed Syria and the remainder of North Africa. The United States stayed out of the grand carving. Only the core of the Empire—Turkey and the ancient city Istanbul—remained in Turkish hands.

The Ottomans were quite literally shell-shocked. How could the mighty German Kaiser and his armies be defeated? It only seemed logical for the Ottomans to side with the strongest power. Unfortunately for them, however, they hadn't counted on the United States's ability to turn the war. Within a year of the US involvement in WWI, German forces were on the retreat. The Treaty of Versailles ended the war in 1918.

Today, it seems that Turkey may once again underestimate the power of the West and back the wrong horse. Turkey, being the geographical descendant of the ancient tribes of Gomer and Beth-Togarmah, has become a strategic ally to Russia. It also harbors ambitious desires for Israel. The evidence can be seen in Turkey's new rise to power, their standing in the Muslim world, and their relationships with other powers.

THE FOURTH QUARTER TURKISH COMEBACK

The old adage, "location, location, location," rings true for Turkey, as it did for any power sitting along the Bosporus. Turkey's location straddles Europe and Asia and sits atop one of the world's premier waterways, the Bosporus Strait. Bordering the Mediterranean Sea and the Black Sea, Turkey is nearly as strategic as Israel. The Byzantines, formerly known as the Eastern Romans, were blessed to have this location centered on the city of Constantinople (now called Istanbul). They held this strategic waterway for nearly 1,000 years after Western Rome was torn apart by wild barbarians.

A small tribe of nomadic Asian horsemen, originally known as the Seljuk Turks, eventually conquered Asia Minor. They battled Christian crusaders in the Holy Land, Byzantine guards in Constantinople, and Persian armies to the east. With the help of giant cannons, the Ottoman Turks finally captured the ancient Byzantine city. For the next 300 years, the Ottoman Turkish Empire dominated the eastern Mediterranean. From Morocco to Iraq, the Balkans to the Sudan, the Ottoman Empire reigned supreme.

Although the Ottoman sultans were also the caliph's of the Sunni Muslim world, they were surprisingly tolerant of other religions. Jews, Christians of every denomination, and even Shiites were often free to practice their own particular religions within the empire.

In the late 15th century, Spain exiled hundreds of thousands of Sephardi Jews (those of Iberian origin) from its country. With nowhere else to go, many of them turned to the Ottoman Empire. According to notable Middle Eastern historian Bernard Lewis, the number of Jews residing in the Ottoman Empire rose dramatically during the early 16th century. The Ottomans opened their borders to them and in return gained valuable firearm technology from them. A 16th century Spanish visitor to the Empire, Vicente Roca, claimed that the Spanish Jews brought the Ottomans knowledge of "brass ordnance," and of "firelocks," which was another word for firearms.[1]

Orthodox Greeks, Armenians, and Bulgarians were allowed to worship freely and were given a certain degree of freedom to run their own affairs. Both Catholic and Protestant Christians found refuge in the vast hinterlands of the Ottoman Empire during the wars of the Reformation and Counter-Reformation. Despite the extra non-Muslim taxes, these religious minorities found a large degree of tolerance in Ottoman lands.

From a political standpoint, the Ottomans had little choice but to maintain their toleration of minority religions. The Balkans were home to millions of Protestant, Orthodox, and Catholic Christians, while eastern Asia Minor and Mesopotamia housed large minorities of Shiites. Greece, Armenia, Bulgaria, and Egypt each had their own large enclaves of Orthodox churches as well.

Ottoman armies seemed unstoppable until a series of setbacks in the late 17th century set the Ottoman Empire on a collision course with itself. In the year 1683, the Ottoman Grand Vizier decided to destroy his ancient enemy Austria. With 250,000 men and enough cannons to knock down every Austrian stronghold, the Ottomans invaded. Turkish forces surrounded Vienna, set fire to its suburbs, and waited for the Viennese to surrender.

Terrified of the Ottomans, the Viennese held out for weeks. Terrified of a Muslim invasion, the rest of Europe reacted quickly. Germans, English, Polish, and Venetians came to the rescue of the beleaguered city and ousted the invading Turks. The Vizier was forced to retreat to Istanbul in shame. For the next two and a half centuries, the Ottomans began a slow retreat into Asia Minor, losing lands to their more powerful neighbors.

Plagued by internal corruption, widespread rebellions, and economic stagnation, the Ottomans were too preoccupied with domestic issues to focus on foreign policy. The harem wives of weak Ottoman Sultans spawned chaos as they battled each other over whose heir would succeed the Sultan. Rather than focusing on battlefield victories, the Janissaries, formerly a fearsome army of slaves which had become a fearful mob of politicians, increased their political prestige and became kingmakers, murdering and deposing unwanted Sultans while installing their own puppets. By the late 19th century, the Ottoman Empire had garnered the nickname "The Sick Man of Europe."

After the debacle of WWI, Turkey reversed its fortunes by becoming the first Muslim country to create a representative democracy. Turkey embraced capitalism, republicanism, and secularism like no other Muslim country ever had. They even wised up by staying away from the Germans in World War II.

Turkey became the most dominant military in the Middle East as well as having the largest economy. Geographically, Turkey is a very tough nut to crack. Surrounded on three sides by water with a mountainous exterior, Turkey is virtually impregnable from land invasion.[2] Any power that controls Turkey has substantial strategic defenses. Blessed by dozens of warm water ports, Turkey has managed to grow its trade as well as naval capabilities.

Turkey sits amidst a region of chaos and division. Syria is currently experiencing a revolution of sorts, the Balkans will be eternally divided and anarchic, and the Caucasus region lacks any rival powers (with the exception of Russia). Only Iran poses any serious threat to Turkey, but their relationship has warmed over the past decade.

Turkey has also seen a drastic change of fortunes economically over the past half century. Because Turkey has maintained its existence as a secular Islamic nation, it is seen as more stable than other Middle Eastern nations. Turkey has received a larger amount of foreign investment as well as tourism because of its lack of radical Islamic sects.[3] Ancient Hittite, Persian, Greek, Roman, Byzantine, and Ottoman ruins lie scattered across Turkey. Its beaches are some of the best in the region, and Turkish industry has surged in recent years. Having made friends with Iran and Russia, Turkey has also gained access to cheap energy. Russia and Iran are Turkey's number one and number two suppliers of energy.[4]

Old Enemies, New Friends

Turkey's ancient foes Russia and Iran have recently warmed up to the Turkish Republic. These relationships have made Western powers nervous for a number of reasons. Iran, for instance, has always been the counterbalance to Turkish power in the region.[5]

The Turkish-Persian rivalry runs deeply through history. From the outset, Turkish Sunni Muslims saw the Shiite Persian dynasties as enemies. Rarely were the Ottomans and the Persians at peace with one another, as they fought continual wars over Mesopotamia for almost 300 years. The Ottomans were at war with the Muslim Persians more than with Christian European powers.

Both the Turks and the Persians have competed for the affections of the Arabs. In turn, the Arabs distrust both powers, but the Turks seem to have the advantage, as most Arabs are Sunni and not Shiite.

During the Cold War, the Turks were solidly in the Western camp as a member of NATO. Turkey was a solid buffer against the Soviets in the Caucasus, while Iran found itself increasingly in the Soviet camp.

In recent years, Turkey and Iran have reached a détente. Both governments have become increasingly anti-Western (Iran much more visibly so than Turkey) and both governments are also very anti-Israel. Turkey and Iran have strong energy ties and a desire to stabilize the Middle East on their own terms.

Turkey's Prime Minister Erdogan is one of the few leaders willing to defend Iran's nuclear program, insisting that it is a peaceful program.[6] The Prime Minister is also one of the only Middle Eastern leaders to have a "working relationship" with Iranian President Ahmadenijad.

As indicated in the previous chapter, Turkey's relations with Russia have warmed tremendously. Long forgotten are the days when Turkish slave traders raided the Russian coasts or when Russian nuclear submarines menaced the shores of the Black Sea. Today, trade, geopolitical strategy, and a keen dislike for the West have cemented Russia and Turkey together in a bond of fellowship.

In addition to natural gas, the Russian government has recently agreed to aid in the development of Turkey as a nuclear power.[7] Turkey's potential as a nuclear power has flown under the radar, as Iran has garnered most of the media attention. A secular, democratic Turkey with nuclear power, firmly in the fold of the West is no threat. An increasingly Islamic Turkey with cooling relations with the West is now becoming a reality.

THE ISLAMIC REPUBLIC OF TURKEY?

Turkey's long struggle with Islamic fundamentalism started during the early days of the Turkish Republic. In 1923, Mustafa Kemal Ataturk, the first president of Turkey and an avowed proponent of secularism, gave ground to the more traditional Muslims of Turkey. Traditional Muslims wanted to change the name of the ancient city of Constantinople, originally named after the first Roman Emperor to legalize Christianity. After some debate, it was renamed Istanbul, meaning "where Islam abounds."

Turkey managed to keep the fundamentalists at bay for the duration of the Cold War, but politics began to change after the fall of the Soviet Union. No longer fearful of a Soviet invasion, Turkey found that it no longer needed the protection of the West. In addition, Turkey was not immune to the growing anti-Western sentiment of most Muslims.

The growing Islamic radicalism of Turkey is illustrated in the rise of the ruling AKP party, also known as the Justice and Development Party. For years Turkey was dominated by secular political parties, keen on keeping religion out of politics. In 2002 the more conservative AKP party defeated the secular parties for the first time and have routed them in every election since. Seen as the epitome of Political Islam, the AKP party is the party of the traditional Turkish Muslim.

The AKP Prime Minister Recep Tayip Erdogan won his third election in a row in 2011. Chris Mitchell of CBN news explained that this election "sparks fears of an Islamic Caliphate."[8] According to political opponents, the AKP party has been accused of restricting freedoms across Turkey, especially the freedom of the press and free speech.[9]

A common theme of conservative Muslim political parties is that of anti-Semitism. In an effort to appease traditional Muslims, Prime Minister Erdogan has distanced himself from Israel. Originally seen as a democratic ally in the region, Israel is now a political target for Turkey. In 2009, Erdogan compared the conditions in the Gaza Strip to a concentration camp.[10] In addition, he called Israel a "persecutor" and halted joint air force exercises with the Jewish nation.[11]

Turkey has also spearheaded the Gaza Flotilla movements of 2011 and 2012. Erdogan's involvement in the flotilla debacle was an effort to "flex his muscles" in the Sunni world. In 2011, Erdogan and his administration demanded that Israel apologize for killing Turkish peace activists on the Gaza Flotilla. When Israeli leaders declined, Turkey expelled the Israeli Ambassador from Istanbul.[12] Being a vocal critic of Israel gained him supporters not only in Palestine but also across the Arab world.[13]

Another popular political move in Turkey is increasing their distance from "the West." The cooling of relations with Europe has been an ongoing occurrence ever since the collapse of the Soviet Union. In addition, the European Union has continually denied Turkey access to union membership for a number of reasons.

Geographically, Turkey is much more Asian than European. The tiny isthmus of Istanbul sits on the European side while the remainder of Turkey sits in Asia Minor. Secondly, the Greek vote continually blocks Turkey's entrance. Greece was dominated by the Ottoman Empire for over 300 years, a memory not easily forgotten. Lastly, the genocide of Armenian Christians by Muslim Turks during WWI was not the best attempt at making friends with Christian Europe. Besides, Turkey has become more reliant on Russia rather than Europe for trade and energy and may eventually tire of European snubs against Turkish membership.

The break with the United States has been more recent and less obvious. Turkey has been estranged from the United States since the 2003 War in Iraq. The war was violently opposed by many in Turkey, and when the United States needed Turkey as a base of operations, they were denied.[14] For the first time in history, a NATO member denied military access to another NATO member, and the United States has not forgotten.

Moreover, Turkish relations with America's enemies have increased significantly. Iran is the most obvious example, but their growing relationship with Russia troubles American policy makers. The same year Turkey suspended its military games with Israel, it invited Syria to join them.[15] Why did they invite Syria? There is no way any nation would willingly choose Syria's military over Israel's except to brazenly insult the quite capable Israeli military. There is still hope for Turkey to mend the break with the West but, as Ezekiel indicated, this may not happen.

Perhaps the most troubling indication that Turkey is becoming increasingly Islamic is the rising accounts of Christian persecutions in Turkey. Christians in Turkey, like other Muslim countries, experience daily hardships for their faith. The reason Turkey has a reputation for tolerance is because of its constitution, which allows freedom of religion. Unfortunately, Christian minorities are not as protected as they should be.

An example is trying to build a new church in Turkey. It is nearly impossible with the government regulation of building permits. Although evangelism is not specifically outlawed, evangelistic Christians are often arrested for "disturbing the peace," or "insulting Allah."[16] Christians in Turkey face confiscation of church property, beatings, and arrests simply for professing faith in Jesus Christ.

In 2007, four Turkish Christians were tortured by a group of young men for three hours before having their throats slit. The torture included disembowelment, stabbings, as well as other unmentionable things. What warranted such a harsh killing? The Christians had invited the group over for a Bible study.[17]

Contrary to the hope of many in the West, Turkey is becoming more traditionally Islamic rather than less. Turkey's relationship with the West and Israel is deteriorating, and persecutions against Christians are on the rise.

TURKEY'S FUTURE PLANS: A NEW OTTOMAN CALIPHATE

In light of recent history, what are some of Turkey's goals? Just from Prime Minister Erdogan's words and actions alone, one can see a plan formulating.

Friedman, among other geopolitical experts, believes that Turkey's government is seeking to broaden their influence amongst Muslim nations, particularly the Arab ones. The Ottoman Empire once dominated the Middle East, and the Turks may seek to do so again. In Erdogan's 2011 victory speech, he proclaimed his victory to be important not only in Istanbul but also in Jerusalem, Damascus, and Sarajevo. All of these cities used to be regional capitals in the old Ottoman Empire.[18] Minister Erdogan would love to see Turkey dominate the Middle East once again as the leader of the Sunni World.

In addition to political dominance, Turkey greatly desires to be the spiritual leader of the Sunni world again. For nearly 400 years, the Arabs bowed to the will of the Sunni Ottoman Caliphs. Recent revolutions and uprisings in Arab countries all have one specific theme in common—the desire for an Islamic caliphate.

Should Egypt or Syria try to initiate a caliphate, it would be nearly impossible. Arab nations are notoriously divided, just as Genesis 16:12 had prophesied. But the Arabs may forget their ancient squabbles and unite under a dominant Turkish caliphate once again.

A caliphate is simply an area under Islamic rule. Historically, laws under caliphates are harsh. During the Arab caliphates of the 7th and 8th centuries, minority religions were given second-class status, Muslims who converted to Christianity were beheaded, non-Muslims were forced to pay higher taxes, and Sharia was the law of the land. Rape victims were stoned to death, along with homosexuals and heretics.

This could never happen in the 21st century—right? Aren't the majority of Muslim nations progressive and peaceful? No! Sharia law is official law in at least twelve countries throughout the Muslim world. The most notorious are Iran, Saudi Arabia, and Sudan. Beheadings and stonings are commonplace in many Muslim nations today.

Sharia law has even crept its way into European society. There are neighborhoods in London where women cannot walk safely without covering their heads. Certain districts of Paris, London, and Amsterdam are off limits to police, allowing the local Muslims to practice Sharia without distraction. The annual riots in Paris may involve some unemployed malcontents, but many of the rioters are newly migrated North African Muslims, angry at France's liberal outlook on life.

The Muslim Sharia concept of "honor killing" is popular in the Middle East, but the United States has seen a few of these occur within its borders. A Muslim honor killing usually involves a husband, father, or brother evoking the name of Allah to kill a wife, sister, or daughter for bringing dishonor to the family. How would the women bring dishonor? Most of the time, an honor killing involves a Muslim female talking with, dating, or seeing a non-Muslim man.

At least seven honor killings have occurred in the United States between 2008 and 2012. No, the OJ Simpson case was not one of them. In 2009, an Iraqi-born man in Arizona ran over his daughter and her non-Muslim boyfriend with his car. The crime? His daughter moved in with a non-Muslim and refused to marry the Iraqi man her father had picked out for her.[19] What is especially unfair is that the daughter never would have had a chance to run over her father with a car as many Muslim cultures forbid women from driving.

In another gruesome case, an Egyptian born man stabbed his seventeen-year-old daughter to death while her mother held her down. Her crime was also dating a non-Muslim boy. Nonetheless, Muslim critics site that honor killings are not mainstream. In a culture where rape victims are often punished, it is not surprising that women find themselves run over by cars. Caliphates can be scary entities indeed, which is why the Western World should worry about the latest happenings in the Middle East.

IS TURKEY FULFILLING PROPHECY TODAY?

Turkey, the geographical descendant of "Beth-Togarmah" and "Gomer," is a regional power once again, and its military and economy are the strongest in the Middle East. It has few rivals in the region and an excellent strategic location. Turkey's relationship with Russia has never been better, and its relationships with Israel and the West have never been worse. Desiring to revive the Ottoman Empire of old and lead the Sunni world under a caliphate, Turkey's joining Russia in an invasion of Israel would be no small stretch.

Chapter Seven

THE PERSIAN MENACE

"And there before me was a second beast, which looked like a bear. It was raised up on one of its sides, and it had three ribs in its mouth between its teeth. It was told, 'Get up and eat your fill of flesh!'" (Daniel 7:5)

Little did Xerxes know that his 480 BC invasion of Greece was nothing more than another attempt by Satan to thwart God's plan for the ages. In Xerxes mind, the destruction of Greece would simply be one more province to add to his empire. He would finally rid himself of Athenian influence in his Greek-speaking provinces, and he would gain considerable plunder.

Satan had much deeper reasons for urging a Persian invasion of Greece. He was going to use the power of the Persian war machine to crush the Greek cities solely for the purpose of altering history and thereby proving God's scriptural prophecies wrong.

Primarily, the absence of Greece would render a huge chunk of Bible prophecy worthless. Without Greece, the prophecies of Daniel would have come to nothing. There would have been no power to counter Persia. The four kingdoms would have never split, making Daniel's prophecies about Alexander and his successor generals mere fairy tales.

The Greek invasion was not the only time Satan has tried this approach. Satan attempted to falsify the prophecies of the Messiah by keeping Jesus from the cross through temptations. In the book of Daniel, he sent a powerful demon, known as the Prince of Persia, to attack a messenger angel for the purposes of keeping the secrets of prophecy from Daniel. From the Romans to the Nazis, Satan has used nearly every world power in futile attempts to destroy the Jewish people, culminating in the Holocaust. The Persian horde would be another attempt to defy God.

Additionally, the prophecies regarding Israel's destruction at the hands of the Romans would not have been fulfilled because the Romans may not have survived the Persian onslaught. Being such a small city at the time, Rome would not have had the power to stop the Persian forces. The future prophecies regarding the Iron beast of the Tribulation would not have come to fulfillment because they would be lacking their Roman foundation.

Secondly, the destruction of Greece would have destroyed what was the foundation of Western civilization. Philosophy, democracy, Greek mythology, mathematic and scientific works, and the Olympics would have perished long ago. In other words, had Persia successfully conquered Greece, Western Civilization would never have existed.

The absence of Greco-Roman culture throughout the Mediterranean would have made the prophecies of Jesus's death on the cross much harder to fulfill. Who would have crucified him, the Persians? Crucifixion was primarily a Roman practice. Persians eventually used it, but only after they borrowed the grisly idea from the Romans.

For the sake of argument, if Jesus had successfully fulfilled the prophecies, paid the price for iniquity and was resurrected, who would have spread his message? Without Greco-Roman culture, Christianity would not have spread so easily.

Greek mythology, although polytheistic, believed deeply in the divine taking the form of man. Greek sculptures of deities were almost always mirror images of men and women. In Greek mythology, the gods were always coming down to earth and taking the forms of humans— for good and for evil. When Paul came to the Greeks with Christ's message that Jesus was God in the form of man, come to redeem them from their sinful ways, it made perfect sense. Why wouldn't God come down in the form of man?

The Greek philosopher Socrates believed that one day the gods would send a redeemer to rescue mankind from their sinful desires. Greek mythology is full of the act of redemption, from Atlas's taking the burden of the world on his shoulders to Hercules's descending into Hades to rescue lost souls.

God also used Roman roads to spread the gospel across the Roman

Empire. Paul traveled across Asia Minor, Greece, Italy, and maybe even Spain, by ship as well as by foot. Yes, Romans persecuted the Christians, but many Roman citizens eventually became followers of Christ.

Without Western civilization, Europe would never have been Western. All of history would have turned out drastically different. There would have been no discovery of the New World (at least by Columbus), no United States, no spreading of democracy across the globe, and who knows, maybe even no NFL.

Without Greece, democracy would have been trampled underfoot by tyranny. The ability of an individual to make a free choice in government or to elect his own leader would have been lost, along with the freedom that democracy naturally breeds. This freedom is one of the most basic themes of the Bible. God originally intended for man to be free. Before the fall, Adam and Eve had free reign over the entire garden. He sent his only Son to free us from the shackles of sin.

Without democracy and freedom, authoritarian dictatorships throughout history would have had an even easier time trouncing religious freedoms, especially Christianity.

Instead, Eastern Persian culture would have flourished. The ideals of the absolute emperor, Zoroastrianism, and total subservience would have been spread. Persian and Arab cultures would be the world's leading powers. Neither society is conducive to Christianity or democracy. Look at the Middle East today. Are there any majority Christian nations in the region? No. Even the minority Christian populations are constantly under attack by their Muslim governments.

As 250,000 Persians descended upon the tiny cities of Greece in the summer of 480 BC, Satan thought he had finally thwarted God. God, however, had raised a rare breed of men solely for the task of stopping the Persian army, and by extension Satan, from any sort of victory—the Spartans. The tale of the 300 Spartans has been passed down through Western culture, made into poems, songs, and movies—frequently exaggerating the truth to enhance the action. Nevertheless, most of the accolades of the Spartans are true.

The Greeks hated being ruled by outside powers. Xerxes had already put down numerous rebellions of Greek cities in Asia Minor, and his father Darius had been humiliated ten years earlier in his botched attempt to invade the Greek cities. Xerxes determined that he would not make the same mistakes of his father. Rather than land on the plains of Marathon, Xerxes planned to land in the north and attack Athens, Corinth, Sparta, Thebes and the other Greek cities from a direction they least expected.

The Persian armies had already destroyed much of northern Greece, pillaging and enslaving as they marched. Despite a terrible storm, which killed many thousands of his men, Xerxes's campaign was going quite well. All that remained was to march through the "Hot Gates," also famously known as the mountain pass of Thermopylae. Once Xerxes passed through the mountains, he could deploy his war machine on the plains and use his overwhelming numbers to crush the Greeks.

Athens was the number one target of the Persian army, and the Athenian people knew it. A number of Athenians fled the city, while its leaders tried to rally enough men to field against the Persians. Cities all over Greece desperately tried to coordinate with one another as to what their battle plan should be.

The King of Sparta knew exactly what to do. Rather than waste time arguing with the Spartan leadership, King Leonidas dispatched a small number of troops, with himself at the head, to the pass at Thermopylae.

The Spartans were drastically different from the rest of Greece in one way—they knew no culture but warfare. Boys were trained to fight beginning at the age of eight, while girls' sole responsibility lay in learning how to raise the best soldiers possible. The Spartans perfected the classic Greek strategy of the phalanx. The phalanx was indeed a powerful strategy, especially when the flanks were protected. A wall of spears and shields, a phalanx operated by thousands of men in unison, was a terrifying sight indeed.

Knowing that the Persians only land route into Greece was through the mountains, King Leonidas, with a grand total of 300 Spartans and 6,000 allies, headed for the mountain pass. The Spartans were met by the largest army they had ever seen. Xerxes brought not only his 10,000 Immortals but also his war elephants from India, Bedouin cavalry from

Arabia, Scythian tribesmen from the north, Nubians and Egyptians from the south, and dozens of other peoples and cultures to the fight.

The Persians had two serious disadvantages. While most of their men were conscripts who had been grudgingly drafted into service, the Spartans fought voluntarily and trained just for the fun of it. Secondly, the pass was only wide enough for twenty men to cross shoulder to shoulder, giving the Spartan phalanx the perfect fighting terrain.

For over a week, the Spartan phalanx held off 250,000 enemy soldiers. Desperate for a quick victory, Xerxes drove his men forward in a futile attempt to break the phalanx. Xerxes had nowhere to retreat, nor could he flank the Spartan phalanx. After a week of fighting, the Spartan's Greek allies left to rendezvous with their own armies, leaving just the 300 Spartans to fend off the Persians.

Eventually, Xerxes managed to find a small mountain pass, enabling him to mount an attack from both sides. Every Spartan at Thermopylae died, but the victory was pyrrhic for Xerxes. He had lost 20,000 men to the small handful of Greeks, and his men were demoralized.

Xerxes eventually captured the city of Athens and put much of it to the flame. Not long after, however, the Greek city-states managed to unite against the remaining Persian invaders. In the ensuing Battle of Platea, the Persian army was forced to retreat to Persia, never to threaten Greece or Western Civilization again. Satan would need to find another way to thwart the will of God.

Today, the Persians are once again being used by Satan in an attempt to defy God. Their President, Mahmoud Ahmadenijad, denies the Holocaust and threatens the extinction of the Jews in Israel. The Ayatollahs who run the country are blatantly anti-Western, as well as anti-Christian. The Persians, more than any of the other nations mentioned in Ezekiel, are bound and determined to be the masters of the Middle East and destroy God's chosen people once and for all.

PERSIAN, NOT MIDDLE EASTERN

Only a handful of countries can geographically trace their ancestry for over 2,000 years; Iran is one of them. In fact, Persians have what Middle

Eastern historian Bernard Lewis describes as "a fierce connection with their past."[1] In antiquity, the Persians laid claim to a vast Middle Eastern empire, and today many Iranians desire to once again rule the Middle East.

Persia has not always had a dislike for the Jews, or the West in general. Cyrus was the deliverer of the Jews, allowing them to return to the Promised Land after their first exile. Xerxes, although he tried to destroy Western Civilization at its inception, was kind to the Jews, allowing his wife Esther to intercede on their behalf.

The Persians, however, have always been different from the rest of the Middle East. For one, they are not Semitic, being neither Arab nor Jewish. Nor are they of Turkic or Egyptian descent. The Persians date their ancestry back to the ancient Aryans, close kin to the Indo-European cultures.[2] In other words, Persians have more common ancestry ties with the Germans and the British than they do with the Arabs.

Secondly, when the Persians converted to Islam, they kept most of their own unique cultural traits and dismissed the Muslim Arab ones, which were deemed too nomadic. Perhaps this is why Persia switched to Shiite Islam in the 16th century. One of the reasons Pan-Arabism never "panned" out was because most Arabs identified themselves as Islamic, both culturally and politically, rather than Arab.[3] Before Islam, the Arabs did not have a vibrant culture. Persia has ancient roots, but they have always been in the same place. When the Persians converted to Islam, they already had thousands of years of cultural history to call their own.

The largest difference between Persia and the rest of the Middle East is not language, ethnicity, or culture but rather their steadfast allegiance to Shiite Islam. Unlike Sunni, Shiite Islam allows Iranians a distinct national identity as well as a religious one.

Shiite Islam can at times be more lenient than Sunni. Although Iran currently practices a form of Sharia law similar to Saudi Arabia, its women have a much greater degree of freedom. The Hijab, or ceremonial covering of the entire body, is not mandatory in Iran as it is in Saudi Arabia. Women in Iran can even become successful, as some females have become doctors and members of Parliament.[4] Iran in no way allows women as much freedom as the West but is better than most Sunni Arab nations.

As the largest Shiite nation, Iran sees itself as the protector of Shiite minorities throughout the world. Roughly twelve to fifteen percent of the Muslim world is Shiite, the vast majority of which live in Iran. Bahrain is over seventy percent Shiite, and Syria, Iraq, and Lebanon have sizable Shiite minorities as well.[5]

Persians are distinctly different from the rest of the Middle East, and this important fact should be taken into account when dealing with the Iranian nation.

From Allies to Enemies

Before the Islamic Revolution of 1979, Iran was America's number one ally in the region. Israel was a crucial spot for democracy, Turkey was an important buffer against Soviet expansion, and Saudi Arabia's oil had its advantages. Iran had the largest army, and a reliable flow of oil (second largest in the Middle East behind Saudi Arabia). The relationship with the Shiite nation began to sour during the 1960s and 1970s. America's "don't ask, don't tell" policy with the Shah of Iran's tactics did nothing to assuage the situation.

Seen as a violent dictator, the Shah of Iran often put down dissent in dictatorial fashion. Because of his strong anti-Communist stance, however, he became a steadfast ally of the United States, and many Iranians began to blame America for keeping him in power.

The American support of Israel was also highly unpopular with traditional Muslim conservatives. Agitated that the holy sites of Jerusalem fell into the hands of the Jews, Iranians began calling Israel "the little Satan," and its protector became known as "the Great Satan."

The Ayatollahs, religious leaders of the country, also condemned the overwhelming flow of Western ideas, fashions, and products into Iran. Bell-bottomed jeans, Hollywood movies, and religious freedom were thought to have come from the devil himself.

Then the tidal wave struck. Revolutionary fervor swept Iran as young people sought to oust their dictator and install an Islamic Republic with the Ayatollahs at the helm. The Shah fled the country, eventually to America, and the Islamic Revolution had begun. Traditional Islamic laws were restored, but anti-Western sentiment continued to fester.

Finally, with the blow that severed the bridge forever, Iranian students stormed the American Embassy in Tehran. Since it was a gross violation of sovereign American territory, the embassy takeover was nothing short of a declaration of war. The Ayatollahs congratulated their zealous students and held the fifty-two Americans hostage for 444 days. Jimmy Carter ordered a rescue attempt, but it was badly botched in the desert, costing the lives of American soldiers. Finally, after Ronald Reagan was elected into office, the Iranians released the hostages. Nevertheless, the damage had been done.

America supported Iraq in the long Iran-Iraq War, but Iran soon found another superpower's support in the Soviet Union. To this day, the Russians still support Iran with cheap weapons, nuclear technology, and natural gas. For the past thirty years, Iran has been one of America's most steadfast enemies. Iran has high hopes for the Middle East, but the plans of Mahmoud Ahmadenijad and the Ayatollahs are much more intricately designed.

PERSIA'S FIVE-STEP PLAN FOR MIDDLE EASTERN DOMINATION

1. SCARE THE LIVING DAYLIGHTS OUT OF THE REST OF THE WORLD

Mission accomplished. Everyone sees right through the Iranian president's excuses for nuclear energy, that is, "we merely want nuclear energy for peaceful reasons." In the very same sentence, however, Ahmadenijad will describe in horrific detail the nuclear destruction of Israel. Is the man crazy? Of course. Would he nuke Israel if he had the chance? Absolutely. But will he? No. A nuclear bomb would destroy the entire nation of Israel, as well as a majority of all Jews on the planet. God's future plan for Israel would not come to fulfillment.

The fact that Iran has not yet tried to bomb Israel leaves geopolitical strategists with three conclusions: Iran does not yet have the bomb,

Ahmadenijad is bluffing, or the Ayatollahs who actually run the country will not allow it. All of Iran's missile tests, nuclear reactors, and uranium production attest to the fact that if they do not have the bomb yet, they may obtain it quite soon. Should this be the case, then reader beware— the end may come even sooner then anyone realized.

Despite Iran's gusto, strategist George Friedman believes that building a nuclear bomb is much harder than it looks,[6] even with Russian help. More than likely, the Iranian president is bluffing in an attempt to "scare the living daylights out of the rest of the world." This theory would fit better with the knowledge that Iran is trying to make itself as unpredictable as possible in order to reach better negotiations with the Western powers.[7]

Nuclear countries can gain a lot more out of negotiations than non-nuclear ones. Somalia, for instance, may very well have the most nutcases on the planet. From time to time, they may send lone terrorists onto American planes, or into American ships, but they could never nuke anyone. No one is afraid of Somalia.

North Korea, on the other hand, has the entire Eastern Pacific on edge. Constantly testing missiles and boasting its nuclear potential, North Korea has their South Korean cousins dying of stress-related diseases. Even China and Russia fear North Korean unpredictability. This allows Kim Jong Il to receive the best negotiations possible. "Fine, fine, take what you want, just don't nuke my country," is usually the reply of his neighbors.

Iran wants to be feared again, which is why it is desperately seeking nuclear weapons. The need to be feared is also why their president constantly reminds the world that Iran could block the Strait of Hormuz, thereby cutting off forty-five percent of the world's oil supply.[8] At any given moment, Iran could order Hezbollah to unleash hell upon Israeli cities with rockets. They could destabilize Iraq in a moment's notice by calling out the Shiite militia groups.

Another indication of how much fun Iranian leaders have instilling fear in everyone around them is found in Shiite apocalyptic theology. Time and again, President Ahmadenijad talks of the 12th Imam and the end of the world. According to Ahmadenijad's brand of Shiite theology, the 12th Imam acts as a Muslim Messiah. His return will usher in a worldwide caliphate of Muslim domination.

In order to bring the 12th Imam, also known as the Mahdi, to power, Shiites must create as much global chaos as possible, hence the nuclear weapons. By provoking a clash of civilizations, the Iranian leader hopes to bring the end-times Mahdi to power.[9] I told you it would be scary.

2. REACH AN AGREEMENT WITH THE AMERICANS ON IRAQ

Iran seeks to dominate the Middle East. The only way Iran can truly become the regional superpower is if the United States's role in the Middle East is drastically reduced. Iranian fear mongering may work in the end. Most geopolitical strategists believe that the United States and Iran will reach an agreement of sorts over the fate of Iraq, as well as the steady output of oil from the Middle East. Studiers of Ezekiel's prophecy also know this to be true.

Ultimately, Iraq will be safe from Iranian aggression. As Revelation and Jeremiah both indicate, the ancient city of Babylon will be rebuilt, and the region around it (Iraq) will become exceedingly wealthy. Perhaps God has used America to protect Iraq from such an Iranian incursion until Iraqi forces are strong enough to defend themselves. In the end, the majority of American troops will leave Iraq, handing off the Iranian problem to the Iraqi government.

The 2003 invasion of Iraq was a smashing success for the American military. Saddam's forces melted away before American tanks and marines. There was, however, nothing peaceful about the peace after the invasion. Iraq exploded. Kurds in the north fought with Shiite and Sunni Arabs in the south in an effort to break away from Iraq. Sunni Baathist loyalists and Shiite militia groups fought each other, as well as American soldiers, in an attempt to seize power. Foreign fighters such as Hezbollah and Al Qaeda streamed through the porous border into the fray.

Iran was the most destabilizing force of them all. Orchestrating Hezbollah units, arming and supplying Shiite militias, and wreaking havoc on Iraqi peace, the Iranian regime was indeed a menace.

It was not until late 2007 that the fighting began to slow, for Saddam's supporters had been largely defeated, the Shiite militia had been brought to the negotiating table, and the foreign Al Qaeda fighters had been killed or repressed. Unfortunately, by destroying Saddam's army the Americans lost the ancient counterweight to Iranian power in the region.[10]

Since that time, the counterweight to Iranian control of the Middle East has been the United States. As the sole superpower, America has too many responsibilities to be a regional counterweight. The American military smashes its enemies, cleans them up, teaches them democracy, and then leaves. Most US combat troops left Iraq in 2012, but there are still many non-combatants supporting Americans still in the region.

If the United States wants to bring the last advisors and contractors home from Iraq, it will have to swallow one of two nasty pills: negotiate with Iran or invade Iran. Since the US military already has significant fighting forces in two other Middle Eastern countries and a NATO bombing campaign in a third, it is highly unlikely that American forces would invade the mountainous plateau of Iran.

Friedman explains that, surprisingly, both countries have a few goals in common. Both countries would like to see the United States leave Iraq permanently. Americans grow war weary quickly and have priorities all over the globe. Iranians, on the other hand, would like to have more influence with the Shiite minority in Iraq without the all-seeing eye of the superpower watching them.[11]

Additionally, both countries would like to see the flow of oil continue. As the world's second largest producer of oil, the Iranians would be hesitant to halt that flow. Yes, Iranian leaders claim they will shut down the Strait of Hormuz, but as a last resort. A stunt like that, although fitting for the Iranian regime, would be counterproductive for them. Lastly, both Iran and the United States fear certain elements of Sunni Islam.[12] Wahhabism, the ideology of Al Qaeda, was a Sunni invention, as are the radical Taliban in Afghanistan.

The détente could go something like this: America could agree to withdraw much of its supporting cast from Iraq, lift economic sanctions, and increase oil purchase from Iran in exchange for Iranian promises to leave nuclear energy alone, leave Iraq alone, leave Israel alone, leave the Gulf States alone, and leave the flow of oil alone. Iran may agree to just about anything in order to get the Americans to leave the region, but as the next points indicate, Iran may break some of their promises.

3. SEIZE BAHRAIN AND BULLY THE GULF STATES INTO SUBMISSION

If there is one nation more terrified of Iran than Israel, it is Saudi Arabia. Saudi Arabia once looked to Iraq as a nice buffer from Iranian aggression, but with the Iraqi military destroyed, the Saudis are more reliant upon the United States than ever before. The Saudis loathe the Iranians. Saudi Arabia is a Sunni Arab monarchy while Iran is a Shiite Persian republic/oligarchy. Until Iraq restores itself, the Saudis are more reliant upon America than ever.

Ezekiel makes it clear that Saudi Arabia will speak out against the invasion but can do little about it. The Saudis will be in the same position when Iran takes over Bahrain and has its way with the other Gulf States. As Scripture indicates, Iraq will eventually prosper and become quite powerful in the region once again, but until that time comes, the Gulf States will continue to be harassed by the Iranians.

Of the Gulf States, analyst Robert Baer believes Bahrain would be the first Gulf State to readily join the Shiite power, as over seventy percent of the population is already Shiite.[13] Bahrain is the perfect acquisition for Iran because the takeover would be largely peaceful. A quick coup of the Sunni royal family ruling Bahrain and the Shiites would have the whole country. Because the takeover will most likely be a peaceful decision by the Bahrainis, the American fleet in Bahrain will have no choice but to sit back and watch.

In 2011, the Shiites of Bahrain revolted against their Sunni masters, desperately seeking a way to overthrow the Sunni monarch. Protesters were violently attacked by the Bahraini regime, and when the protests grew, the king of Bahrain hit the panic button, allowing Saudi tanks to roll into the tiny nation. The protests died down after dozens of Bahrainis were killed by Saudi forces.

As for the other Gulf States, any attack on them would obviously put Iran back on the radar and illicit an angry response from the West. So why would the Iranians risk an American incursion back into the region? It is possible that the Iranians are slowly running out of oil. In 1974, Iran was pumping out 6 million barrels of oil a day, compared to 1.5 million barrels a day in 2007.[14] Are the Iranians just sitting on their oil, willingly hurting their economy just to save it? Doubtful. Should their position as an oil king become threatened, the Iranians will undoubtedly take desperate measures.

After they have attained Bahrain, it is very unlikely that Iran would invade any other Arab nation. Western retaliation may be too much of a gamble for the Persians to invade by force. Instead, Iran may resort to their old ways, infiltrating Arab nations by supporting Shiite militias and paramilitary groups such as Hezbollah and bullying them into advantageous oil deals.

4.   MAKE FRIENDS WITH OTHER ANTI-AMERICAN NATIONS

On a global scale, Iran does not have very many friends. Most people do not take kindly to being threatened with nuclear holocaust. The friends Iran does have are wacky indeed. What do Iran and Venezuela have in common? They share nothing except their shared hatred for America and the West. Yet the two leaders get together quite often to rant and rave against America. Danny Glover even joins them from time to time.

Regionally, the Iranian regime has a good relationship with Syria and has been working on a newfound friendship with an old enemy—Turkey. Despite their opposing religious views, the Sunni Turks and the Shiite Persians find each other on the same side. Although Iran's hatred for Israel is more visible, Turkey's anti-Semitism has grown steadily over the years.

Turkey has benefited greatly from oil deals with Iran, and as the two largest regional powers in the Middle East, these two nations can overlook their differences to provide some semblance of stability to the region.

Both countries have a strong desire to restore their old empires in the Middle East. If attaining their goals includes temporarily using each other, so be it. Both countries see themselves as the natural leaders of their Muslim branches, and both countries strongly desire control of the Islamic holy places: Mecca, Medina, and Jerusalem. As Ezekiel indicated in his prophecies, the Turks and the Persians may cooperate to achieve their goals but will eventually turn on each other, as well as the Russians.

Over the past thirty years, the Russians have been one of Iran's most steadfast allies. The Soviet Union has consistently skirted embargoes and sanctions against the rogue nation. The tit for tat of oil for nuclear technology has sealed the bond between these two nations. I am also convinced that we will soon see Ahmadenijad joining Putin in shirtless horseback riding together.

Russia's continued anti-Western rhetoric sends chills of glee down Ahmadenijad's leg. Not only that, but it seems that Russia takes pride in circumventing American tactics with Iran. Embargoes and sanctions cannot work if a large country like Russia breaks the rules. With Russia's help, the Iranian nuclear program will continue to flourish.

5.   SEIZE QUD AND THE MUSLIM HOLY PLACES

Everyone knows the city of Mecca, but what is the city of Qud? Qud is a common Iranian reference to the city of Jerusalem. One of the Revolutionary guard's special units is called the "Qud Force."[15] The primary goal of the Qud Force is the restoration of "Qud" into Shiite Muslim hands. Shiite Persians have never controlled Jerusalem, but they would quickly take advantage of any opportunity to do so.

In recent decades, the Iranians have been solidifying ties with the radical Palestinian group Hamas. Since 2001 especially, Sunni Hamas has grown closer to the Shiite power.[16] Despite their religious differences, Hamas and Iran have one common enemy in Israel. Iran is also the number one supplier of weapons to Hamas.[17]

Despite Ahmadenijad's threats of nuclear attacks, a nuclear holocaust is not his plan. A nuclear attack of Israel would not only obliterate the tiny country and put the prophecies of Israel in jeopardy, but it would also destroy one of Islam's holiest cities. Besides, the Ayatollahs call the shots and would never allow Jerusalem to be completely destroyed. The

Iranian regime does not want to destroy Israel; it just wants to surgically remove all Jews from the land. A land invasion with Iranian troops would be the only way to accomplish this task.

After Iran and Turkey split up the city of Jerusalem and Russia seizes strategic ports and industrial complexes inside Israel, the Iranians may focus on occupying Mecca and Medina, only a few hundred miles from the Israeli border. By the time Saudi Arabia recovered from the shock of seeing Israel destroyed, it would be too late to defend the Muslim holy cities.

IS IRAN FULFILLING THE PROPHECIES OF EZEKIEL TODAY?

Ahmadenijad does little to cloak his weekly diatribes against the nation of Israel and the Great Satan. It is obvious that the Iranian regime despises both the West and Israel. But could they be close to joining a potential invasion of the tiny country alongside Russia and Turkey?

Iran, like Turkey and Russia, has the military power to accomplish such a feat. Iran has never been closer to Russia. Any Russian attempts on Israel would be met with enthusiasm by Iran. Turkey, the historic Sunni enemy of Persia, has significantly warmed their ties with Iran by putting aside their Sunni/Shiite rivalry. With a cowed Arab populace, a weak Iraq, and a lackluster response from the West, an Iranian invasion today would be very possible.

Desiring the cultural and political power of controlling Jerusalem and destroying the Jews, Iran has both the means and the motivation to invade Israel today. Syria would gladly open the way through the Golan Heights, and the Iranians, marching alongside the Russians and the Turks, will also meet their end.

Chapter Eight

EAST AFRICAN CONUNDRUM

Persia, Cush and Put will be with them, all with shields and helmets. (Ezekiel 38:5)

The Bible is accurate…Ezekiel did not botch the prophecy when he added the East African regions of "Cush" and "Put." Today, this region is rife with corruption, starvation, genocide, and internal warfare. The nations of Sudan, Ethiopia, Somalia, and Eritrea are perhaps some of the least visited countries in Africa, perhaps even on earth (other than by peacekeepers or Red Cross workers). Additionally, they are also some of the poorest nations on earth. The greatest threat they pose is to themselves. Should any of these countries organize itself and join the Russians it would be surprising indeed, but perhaps not as surprising if one understands the history of the region.

Sub-Saharan Africa is home to the highest AIDS percentages, the lowest life expectancies, and some of the most corrupt governments in the world. Yes, the wild life is spectacular, but starvation, bad water, and chronic diseases are a common problem for many in the region. This was not always so.

The ancient Nubians from southern Egypt and the Sudan were a dominant African kingdom that eventually conquered Egypt in the 9th and 8th centuries BC. Borrowing heavily from Egyptian culture and religion, the Nubians even built their own pyramids. Rich in gold, diamonds, and ivory, the Nubian culture was one of the wealthiest of the ancient world.

On the other side of the continent, the horsemen of Numidia plagued Romans and Carthaginians alike. King Jugurtha kept the Roman legions at bay for a number of years before he was finally captured and executed in the 1st century BC. The Ancient Ethiopians, known as the Axumites, led a vibrant culture to the south of Nubia, while the kingdoms of Ghana and Zimbabwe thrived with large trading empires to the south and west.

As Europeans were sailing across the seas and printing books, many African cultures were stuck reminiscing their glory days. It did not help that Arab slave traders from the north introduced one of history's most hideous practices—African slavery. Initially, Arab slavers would capture unsuspecting villages, but they soon capitalized on the ancient tribal grudges most African villages had long held. Soon Africans were enslaving Africans, selling them down the rivers to Arab slave traders who in turn sold African slaves to the Europeans.

Over ten million African slaves found themselves displaced from Africa and transplanted into the New World. Over three hundred years later, the slave trade had ended but African cultures had not recuperated, especially those in the western and eastern regions closest to the sea. By the 19th century, European missionaries, soldiers, diplomats, and engineers drove deeply into Africa colonizing, modernizing, and evangelizing the continent. For better and for worse, Africa would never be the same.

For the better, Africa became the most Christianized continent in the world. Africa experienced the largest and fastest conversions to Christianity ever recorded. In 1910, only nine percent of the sub-Saharan population was Christian—by 2010 it had risen to sixty-three percent.[1] Europeans also built Africa an infrastructure complete with railroads, telephone poles, hospitals, and bridges.

For the worse, however, the democratic nations of Europe forgot to treat African nations democratically. Europeans ran the continent without much input from the indigenous populations. Moreover, for the European rivals Africa became another notch in the belt, a land rich in raw resources.

When European nations left in the mid 20th century, all hell broke loose in Africa. Much like the apocalypse that would consume the world should America's stabilizing effect disappear, the disappearance of a stabilizing European presence set off episodes of violence across Africa.

In the south the minority white populations were left in charge of vast territories, enacting a segregation system known as Apartheid and holding millions of Africans in second-class status. In the rest of the con-

tinent, ancient rivalries broke loose, embroiling the continent in inter-
mittent civil wars and genocides.

Secondly, most African leaders lacked the experience to run effective
modern governments. Many African nations soon found themselves with
corrupt government officials. George Friedman explains that the concept
of a nation/state is largely foreign to most African tribes.[2] Africa is a land
of many peoples, but few actual nations. According to Friedman, after
Africa undergoes more civil strife and more warfare, actual nations will
evolve out of the mess of the continent.[3]

It was during the colonial era of African history that Islamic extremism was introduced to the continent. Ever pushing southward, Islam had
conquered much of sub-Saharan Africa. The radical elements of Wahhabi
Islam gave many of the disaffected masses an outlet for their anger and
hatred, with some directed at the West. Nowhere in Africa was this more
prevalent than the Sudan.

THE RISE OF ISLAMIC EXTREMISM IN EAST AFRICA

In the summer of 1881, the Mahdi finally came to Sudan. The famous
end-times Imam had come to rescue the Islamic world and restore a
caliphate across the land. Although laughed at by the Ottoman Caliph
in Istanbul, the Mahdi was quite popular amongst the poorer masses of
East Africa. Also known as Muhammad Ahmad, the Mahdi was a native
Sudanese Dervish, or Arab tribesman. He despised the Western rulers of
the Sudan and sought to drive them from Sudan and Egypt, and later
the entire Middle East.

At the time, Sudan was ruled by the Egyptian military. Egypt, on the
other hand, was both part of the Ottoman Empire and a protectorate of
the British Empire. In other words, Sudan had three overlords.

The Mahdi made his public statement just as the British had begun
to crack down on the slave trade in the region, a popular tradition
amongst Arab Dervishes. Knowing the British attempt to ban slavery was
incredibly unpopular amongst conservative Muslims, the Mahdi rallied
his tribesmen together and initiated a revolt against Egyptian/British rule.
Using his Wahhabi background to appeal to the conservative tribesmen,

the Mahdi gained a sizable following. The Mahdi's goals were simple: drive out the Western invaders, purify Islam back to its traditional roots, and restore the caliphate.

In 1882 blood was spilt as the British deployed two Egyptian armies into the deserts of Sudan to destroy the Mahdi's army. Both Egyptian armies were annihilated. Large swaths of territory were quickly falling under the Mahdi's control, and only the regions around Khartoum still opposed the Sudanese prophet. Rather than involve themselves in a small, regional war, the British government chose the less courageous route—appeasement.

The British had not taken the wild-eyed desert prophet seriously yet decided to evacuate all British and other foreigners from Sudan, just in case. To carry out the evacuation they sent the famous war hero General "Chinese" Gordon to Khartoum. Upon his arrival in Sudan, Gordon realized the gravity of the situation. Should the Mahdi successfully drive Westerners out of the Sudan, he could potentially launch an assault on Egypt. Every fundamentalist radical from Rabat to Karachi would rise up against their Western rulers and restore the Arab caliphates of old. Instead of fleeing, Gordon manned the ramparts of Khartoum, putting up a strong defense against the Mahdi's army.

The British government sent an army to relieve the beleaguered city, but they arrived a few days too late. In 1885, the Sudanese rebels stormed the city's walls and beheaded General Gordon, displaying his head on a pike for all to see. The message was simple—this is what happens to anyone who tries to stop the advance of pure Islam.

The British were distraught as to how they should respond. Much like America's response to Islamic terrorism before 9/11, the British did nothing. Instead, they continued their retreat into Egypt and closed the door on trade down the Nile River, quite literally sticking their heads in the sand.

Soon after his victory at Khartoum, the charismatic leader died of typhus. Ironically, had the Mahdi been able to access Western hospitals and medicine he so despised, he might have lived. It was also rumored that one of his jealous harem girls murdered him in the middle of the night.

Despite having lost their leader, the Mahdist forces continued to intimidate and enslave the local Christian tribes of Sudan. In 1896, the British finally decided to retaliate. British General Lord Kitchener, at the head of 23,000 British and Egyptian soldiers, howitzers, maxim guns, and warships, led an assault on the Wahhabi strongholds of Sudan.

By 1898, the British had captured nearly all of the Mahdist strongholds, with the exception of Omdurman. All the British needed to end the uprising was a decisive victory against the Madhist army. Fifty thousand Dervishes and Sudanese tribesmen rallied to the last stronghold at Omdurman, where they prepared for the British attack.

In one of the most quintessential clashes between Islam and the West, the Battle of Omdurman highlighted the vast technological differences between the two societies. General Kitchener, knowing the rebel's affinity for offense, set up a defensive position along the waters of the Red Sea. Warships to his rear, and Maxim guns at the front, the British army had the best weaponry technology had to offer. Before the battle commenced, Kitchener was heard to have said, "Whatever happens, we have the Maxim gun and they have not."

The Sudanese, on the other hand, were comprised of two main troops: Arab Dervish cavalry and Sudanese infantry, also called "fuzzy wuzzies" by the politically incorrect British. Fuzzy Wuzzy was a common description for the large, unkempt mass of hair atop their heads—typically, a large Afro gone wild.

The Sudanese were not to be mocked. Having organized the largest army in Sudan's history, the Mahdist forces were fearless and motivated. Armed with rifles, scimitars, spears, and long swords, the Sudanese were superior to the British in hand-to-hand fighting. Mahdist troops had also captured a great number of British cannons in previous victories.

But Kitchener knew not to let the Sudanese get too close. Using their superior firepower, Kitchener's British and Egyptians wiped out over 15,000 Sudanese in a matter of minutes. The British only experienced 500 casualties after a brave but foolish cavalry charge. Omdurman was not only a lopsided victory for the West, but it was also the last time an

Islamic army challenged the supremacy of Western civilization on an open field of battle.

Instead of challenging the power of Western militaries, fundamentalists such as Osama Bin Laden and Al Qaeda have sought to attack the West with fear and surprise. Radicals have learned that using small cells of men to coordinate terrorist attacks on civilian targets is far more effective than suicidal charges against Maxim guns and warships.

When a future large power such as Russia, combined with the Muslim militaries of Turkey and Iran, seek to invade and destroy Israel, Wahhabis across the globe may join the invaders on the open field of battle against Israel.

SUDAN TODAY

Sudan is still the wild west of East Africa. Run by a cabal of corrupt Islamists, Sudan is one of the world's premier Sharia states. Strict Islamic law rules the land. The Southern Sudanese tribes of the south, particularly in Darfur, have experienced tremendous persecution from the Arab Muslim government. Sunni militia groups, sanctioned by the government, initiated violent genocidal killings against the Christian Sudanese during the 1990s.

With no end in sight, Sudan looks to continue its run as one of the worst countries in the world. It would be no small stretch of the imagination for Sudanese Muslims to again be enticed by a charismatic, radical Wahhabi prophet bent on the destruction of Israel.

ETHIOPIA: OLDEST CHRISTIAN SOCIETY IN AFRICA...FOR NOW

The Ethiopian Orthodox Church is indeed one of the oldest Christian institutions in Africa. With roots that stretch back to the New Testament, Ethiopia has a proud Christian heritage. Legend claims King Solomon's beautiful visitor, the Queen of Sheba may have originated from Ethiopia. What would possibly possess Ethiopia to attack Israel alongside the Russians and Islamic radicals?

Despite a large Jewish population and a long history of Christianity, Ethiopia has a troubled past with the West. Attacked by Italy during

Europe's 19th century scramble for Africa, Ethiopia has long held a reservation towards the West. With the help of their mountainous terrain and centralized army, the Ethiopians withstood Italy's first attempt. In 1935, the Italians under Mussolini invaded Ethiopia—this time with tanks. With the onset of WWII, the Italians eventually left but gave the Ethiopians a bad taste for Italian dictators.

For some reason Russia has always taken a liking to Ethiopia. Russia was one of the few nations to publicly denounce the Italians in the 1930s, and even offered Ethiopia supplies and aid.[4] With the help of Russian support, Ethiopia became a de facto Communist nation in the 1970s and 1980s. Ethiopia's dabbling in Communism may be one of the reasons its economy and infrastructure are such a wreck today.

In recent years, Ethiopia has been one of the poorest, famine-wrecked nations in the world. Nevertheless, the Russians have still made large investments in the region. Russia is seeking to create a new economic zone in east Africa, ironically pinpointing the nations of Ethiopia, Sudan, and Somalia.[5] These are the very nations mentioned in Ezekiel as joining Russia in the future. Despite assistance from Russia, Ethiopia still maintains a terrible poverty level, with little hope for the future.

A second possibility as to Ethiopia's participation in the future invasion is their growing Islamic minority. Muslims first began trickling into the mountainous country in the 7th century, shortly after the rise of Islam. Ethiopia maintained its existence as a largely Christian nation until this past century. Today, almost half of Ethiopia, roughly forty-five percent, adheres to the Muslim faith.[6]

Unlike the Western world, Ethiopia's birthrates are still soaring. By 2050, Ethiopia's population will reach 145 million.[7] If Islam grows half as fast in Ethiopia as it does in any other country it invades, Ethiopia will soon become one of the largest Muslim nations in Africa. Residing so close to Al Qaeda hotspots such as Yemen and Somalia, it should come as no surprise that Ethiopia may one day find itself radicalized.

Somalia: Wahhabi Muslim Paradise

Somalia makes Ethiopia seem like an efficiently run, modernized state.

That is because Somalia has no government. Since the early 1990s, Somalia has been run by violent warlords. Each government that attempts to control and tame the wild nation finds itself under siege in Mogadishu by angry hordes of young, unemployed, radicalized Somalis.

During the late 19ᵗʰ century, the Italians and British managed to keep some semblance of peace between the warlords. Unfortunately, upon their departure Somalia's ability to govern itself declined rapidly. Today, most of Somalia's citizens practice Sharia law with all of its tyrannical practices.

In the late 1980s, Somalia had a famous visitor: Osama bin Laden. In Somalia, bin Laden found numerous recruits to his Al Qaeda cause. He even taught local militia groups how to shoot down American helicopters. These militias put their practice to the test during the 1993 UN-American debacle famously portrayed in the movie *Blackhawk Down*.

During the 1990s, rival Somali warlords seized UN cargoes of food and distributed it only to their followers. President Clinton ordered the seizure of the strongest Somali warlord, Mohammad Farra Aidid. The routine arrest of a local thug turned into three days of vicious urban warfare when Somali militias attacked American forces.

Pinned down, Americans were unable to rescue downed Blackhawk helicopter pilots, and the local UN peacekeeping force was incompetent. The world watched CNN in horror as manic Somalis danced on the naked bodies of dead American soldiers, then hanged them from bridges.

Finally, after eighteen Americans and almost 1,000 Somalis were killed, UN tanks rolled in to rescue the wounded and exhausted American troops. The tragedy officially ended when Somali militias agreed to return their hostage, an American pilot. But instead of instilling "shock and awe" into the Somali populace, Americans practiced the counterproductive tactic of "turn and run." In 1993, America abandoned Somalia to her own wild desires. It was Somalia that emboldened Al Qaeda terrorists to expand their war against America, culminating in 9/11.

Today, Somali radicals are once again emboldened by Western apathy, with many young men taking to the high seas in acts of piracy. Unlike the days of the Barbary pirates, modern Somali pirates dash up in sleek, fast speedboats armed with .50 caliber machine guns. All but the most foolhardy merchant vessels are forced to give up their cargoes. Many find themselves taken hostage for weeks and sometimes months until their governments can ransom them.

Where might Somalis find such sophisticated weaponry? The Russian black market traders have gladly sold weapons to Somalia, so long as Russian ships are not targeted. The Russian government itself has strong desires for Somalia simply for the geostrategic wealth it could bring.

Somalia sits along one of the world's most heavily traveled waterways. Oil tankers heading to the East make their way through the Suez Canal, down the Red Sea, and through the Gulf of Aden into the Indian Ocean. Just like the Strait of Hormuz, the Gulf of Aden is also valuable for the same oil shipping purposes. Somali pirates have exploited this crowded waterway and the Russians see the strength in owning such a strip of land.

COULD EAST AFRICAN NATIONS JOIN RUSSIA TODAY?

Out of greed, desperation, and hatred for Israel and the West, Sudan, Somalia, and eventually Ethiopia may all jump at the chance to take "plunder." Russian weaponry, money, or food may be all it takes to entice the people of this strategic region of the world into joining their armies.

Although none of these African nations is in the least bit powerful, many of their people are devout followers of Wahhabi Islam, one of the purist forms of Islam on the planet. Another wild-eyed Mahdi could step up and rally Islamic fanatics in the region to attempt to reclaim Jerusalem on behalf of Allah.

Chapter Nine

THE MERCHANTS OF TARSHISH: DIVIDED YET POWERFUL

Sheba and Dedan and the merchants of Tarshish and all her villages will say to you, "Have you come to plunder? Have you gathered your hordes to loot, to carry off silver and gold, to take away livestock and goods and to seize much plunder?'" (Ezekiel 38:13)

Ezekiel's phrase "merchants of Tarshish," also mentioned in Isaiah and Jonah is a collective phrase for "lands of the far west." In the Old Testament, these lands extended to what was then Spain, England, and Western Europe. Today, the descendants of the merchants span the globe. From the United States to Australia, the descendants of Tarshish can be found in every corner of the world.

Even Daniel saw that European power would always be curbed by their inability to unite. Europeans were known to Daniel as the feet and toes of "iron and clay." The iron represents Europe's descent from Rome, including their government, culture, and military superiority, whereas the clay represents the fact that Europe has always been a very diverse place.

From time to time, Europe has managed to unite itself under various economic unions, most famously, the European Union. Europe and the Western world will once again unite in opposition to Russia's invasion of Israel. Politically, Europe has not been united since the days of the Romans and will remain divided until the antichrist takes over the Western world. Until that time, European attempts at unity will fail just as spectacularly as they have in the past.

The key to uniting Europe under one government is the acquisition, voluntarily or involuntary, of Great Britain. Kings and dictators throughout European history realized they could never become master of Europe without conquering Britain.

In the late 16th century, the Spanish king Philip II already controlled a vast New World empire, as well as large portions of the low countries and Italy. Philip II's attempt to conquer England ended in disaster in 1588. When the Spanish Armada sought to land troops in southern England, it was met by one of the worst storms in English history. The storm ravaged Spanish warships, sending some ships as far off course as northern Scotland. The hapless Spaniards that landed in Scotland were immediately killed by the wild Scotsmen. The luckier ships were blown off-course to Ireland, where hatred of the English ran strong, and the invaders were given food and shelter.

The English navy managed to finish off any ships the storm did not destroy. England was not to become another domain of Spanish rule. From that point on, the Spanish Empire began to crumble. The Armada cost Philip millions in Spanish gold and silver, never to be replaced.

Two hundred and fifty years later, Napoleon tried a different approach. Unable to defeat the British navy on the seas, Napoleon landed troops in Egypt in an attempt to choke off British trade from its colonies. With Egypt under control, Napoleon could then capture trade ships from India and China. The Egyptian plan failed when British warships bottled the French expeditionary force in the Nile Delta, destroying the French supply fleet.

When the Egyptian campaign failed, Napoleon spent the next ten years conquering most of continental Europe, and bullying the remaining powers—Russia, Prussia, and Austria—into submission. Still unable to invade England, Napoleon instituted a continental trade embargo against Britain. Every country in Europe was outlawed from trading with the island nation.

The Russians balked at losing access to finely made British goods, and they made their defiance known to Emperor Napoleon. As a result, Napoleon invaded the massive nation with 500,000 men. After two harsh years of fighting, freezing, starving and dying, Napoleon and his army returned to Poland with 40,000 men, less than 1/10 of his original army.

To add insult to injury, after Napoleon's return from exile, his last grasp at European domination met its end against Prussian and British troops on the battlefield of Waterloo. On a side note, the Russians continued trading with Britain.

The most recent attempt to unite Europe by defeating Britain was led by Adolf Hitler and his Nazi regime. Having conquered Poland in weeks and France in a month, Hitler then systematically added every European nation to his Third Reich. Only Britain held out.

Despite all of his air attacks, Hitler could not conquer Britain without his Blitzkrieg warfare. The German military's success lay in its ability to pound enemies quickly with multiple weapons. First, an air campaign would blast enemy planes from the skies while a bombing campaign destroyed important military and industrial complexes. Second, the Germans would quickly invade the region with infantry, tanks, and other mechanized transport. Britain was spared because of the detached nature of their geography; an island cannot be attacked by tanks and infantry.

Europe today is still divided, and Britain even more so than the rest. For one, Britain's biggest ally is not a country in Europe but rather their ex-colony, the United States of America.

Anglo-American Relationship

America, as an extension of Great Britain, is still considered a merchant of Tarshish, and the largest of her "young lions." In culture, heritage, and policy, the Americans and British find themselves on the same side of the table. French and German critics have often labeled Britain the fifty-first state of the US.

Culturally, America and Britain share the same language, heritage, Protestant form of Christianity, and they equally cherish freedom and independence. Americans and Britains share a love for rock music, tea, and witty humor as well.

The British, more independent minded than most Europeans, kept their currency when most others in the EU abandoned their own for the Euro.

Calls for the liberation of Iraq were expressed not only by President Bush but also by British Prime Minister Tony Blair. Together, the British and the Americans defeated the Nazis, overpowered the Soviets, and ousted Saddam. Over the past decade, American and British forces fought alongside one another in Afghanistan, and assisted each other in the bombing campaign in Libya.

Politically, the British are more liberal-minded than America, but this does not change the fact that the British will usually follow the lead of America rather than Germany or France. The British realize what the French and Germans grudgingly will not admit: European prosperity swivels around American power.

EURO-AMERICAN RELATIONSHIP

If Europe were united, it would have more people, resources, and economic power than the United States. Even in the Euro's best days, the European Union still could not counter American economic or military power. When they are united under a common cause, however, Europe and America are unmatched. Today, they represent, as analyst Brzezinski claims, the "global core of power and wealth."[1] Despite the recent economic crises that have overtaken the continent, Europe will not lose its economic clout in the world. The Euro as a currency may well disappear, but its collapse will leave behind a continent no worse than before the EU was invented, and the continent might well be stronger than before.

Since the 16th century, Europeans have dominated economically and militarily. The acquisition of two massive landmasses in the New World only furthered their power. New World/Old World relationships, especially with the United States, created the beginnings of a global economy, and the European/American dynamic has reigned ever since.

Although divided by cultural differences and a massive ocean, the two powers, Europe and America, work best when concerted together. As the inventor of globalization, Europe's clout and economic power helps America maintain stability throughout the world. Should European nations consistently undermine American authority, the task would be much more difficult. In other words, the United States would lose its omnipotence without Europe's help.[2]

Without America's protection, Europe would become a toothless tiger. Russia would have a much easier time intimidating individual European countries. Moreover, divided as European militaries are, they would lack the military power to curb Russian aggression.

Throughout the coming years, and even through the future Russian invasion of Israel, America and Europe will find themselves on the same side, verbally, if not more so, opposed to the Russo-Islamic powers. Only one country in Western Europe may find itself, for the first time in history, on the side of the Russians—Germany.

THE GERMAN QUESTION

Germany has never quite found its niche in Europe. France is the cultural elitist. Italy is the fashion snob. Spain and Portugal are the lazy nephews. Greece is the hothead. Ireland is the drunk. Switzerland is the neutral peacemaker. Russia is the outsider. The Balkans are the troublemakers. The Netherlands are the potheads. The Scandinavian countries are the aging grandparents. The Eastern Europeans are the new workaholics, and Britain is the distant uncle that only comes home for Christmas. But Germany is the overworked and underappreciated stepchild of Europe.

For one, Germany lacks the Roman ancestry of the rest of Western Europe, yet it is still considered to be a Western power. When Roman legions marched into the forests of Germany in 15 AD, German barbarians massacred them in one of the worst Roman defeats of their time. The Germans desired autonomy over roads, aqueducts, and theaters. Later, parts of Germany were Romanized, but most of the country was not.

Evidence of a lack in Roman heritage can be seen by Germany's distaste for democracy. The Weimar Republic, a weakened government after WWI, failed to protect Germany from the twin terrors of inflation and starvation. Soon, Hitler and the Nazis came to power and ended the brief stint with democracy. Only after WWII did West Germany embrace democracy. East Germans have only had democracy for a couple of decades.

In addition to the lack of Roman ties, Germany consistently breaks with the rest of European trends and traditions. Never quite fitting in, Germans march to the beat of their own drum. When France, England,

and Spain were unifying under powerful monarchs in the Middle Ages, Germans concentrated their political and economic power in urban cities. Rather than centralize their power, they elected their Princes and remained a loose confederation of cities and states.

In 1517 when Martin Luther posted his Ninety-five Theses on the doors of the All Saints Church of Wittenberg, Germans supported the move by protecting Luther from the Catholic inquisition. They also started the Protestant Reformation, again breaking away from the rest of Catholic Europe.

As other European powers throughout the 18th and 19th centuries were preoccupied with colonizing, the Germans were busy perfecting one of their best cultural achievements: warfare. Germany's obsession with all things military does not necessarily separate it from the rest of Europe, but German generals throughout history fielded the best armies.

The history of Prussian, and eventually German, military prowess unnerved France, Russia, and Britain so much that they combined forces not once, but twice to defeat Germany. WWI began largely as an arms race between Germany and the rest of Europe. Germany, unsure of itself and its place in Europe, felt threatened by France and Russia. France and Russia were perhaps more afraid of Germany than the Germans realized. A complex web of alliances eventually pulled not only Europe but also the rest of the world into the Great War.

World War II began where World War I ended, with the German question still unanswered. Hitler used all the German unease he could find to build the Third Reich. Unlike the French and British empires of the past, the new German Empire was brutal. Nazi death camps systematically wiped out nine million people, two-thirds of which were Jews. Again, Germany broke with the European liberal approach to toleration by slaughtering millions of people.

After the Nazi Empire fell apart, Germany was split between capitalism and communism, freedom and dictatorship. The Communist Russians were not kind to Germany, and the German question would have to wait until the fall of Communism in the early 1990s.

Today, Germany continues to question its role in Europe. Germany has become the obvious economic leader of the European Union and fields the largest and best-equipped army. German technology and automobiles are some of the best in the world. Who doesn't like BMW's or Mercedes Benz?

Over the past few decades, Germany has been a solid ally of both the United States and the rest of Europe, putting its warlike past behind. In recent decades, however, entreaties by the Russians have begun to pull Germany and Russia closer than they have ever been before. The main bond between the two nations involves energy and technology deals. As stated previously, most of Germany's energy comes from Russia, and a great bulk of Russia's energy goes to Germany, roughly twenty percent of its natural gas and ten percent of its oil.[3] In exchange, Germany provides Russia with technology products.[4] Despite years of warfare and suspicion, the two nations are coming together in an economic alliance.

This newfound friendship has caused a rift between Germany and the United States. Chancellor Merkel is hesitant to upset the Russians, yet she also desires to continue the working relationship with America. Evidence of the rift can be seen in America's Middle Eastern policy.

Germany, like France and Russia, opposed the war in Iraq. The Germans, being the largest European member of NATO, have put forth the lowest percentage of troops to the fights in Afghanistan and Libya. American policy makers argue that Germany is not carrying its NATO weight.[5]

Geopolitical analysts believe the rift between the United States and Germany will only continue as long as Russia's energy pressure continues to envelope Germany. Moreover, the Germans grow weary of being the economic workhorse of the European Union. They may decide to break the trend, pulling away from the rest of Europe and moving into the Russian camp.

EUROPE'S FUTURE

The Scriptures tell readers a number of events that will drastically affect Europe: the Russian invasion of Israel, the fruition of the global governance movement, and the coming of the antichrist, to name a few.

First, Germany's opposition to the Russo-Islamic invasion of Israel may not be complete, as Germany may seek to align itself with Russia. At the very least, the Germans may pressure the Western World, including America, into neutrality because of Germany's addiction to Russian energy. Western Europe and America may not succumb to the pressure, but German insistence might be great.

Second, the coming global government, foretold by Daniel in his book and John in Revelation, is largely a European idea. The United Nations, founded by Europeans after WWII, was the offspring of the League of Nations and was designed to instigate and promote a global community, with the Western world in charge. NATO, IMF, and the Global Monetary Fund are all European attempts to organize and fashion the world to Europe's liking. No wonder American's aren't too keen on the United Nations.

Even the ages of imperialism and colonialism foreshadowed a global world headed by Europeans. In the late 19th and early 20th centuries, nearly ninety percent of the world was inhabited or controlled by Europeans and their offspring. The British, French, Dutch, Portuguese, Italians, Germans, and Russians colonized the world. Even the tiny nation of Belgium owned millions of square miles in central Africa, known today as the Republic of Congo.

Colonialism was the European attempt to unite the world by force and under their leadership. Today, that same idea still tickles the European fancy. In the future, Europeans may fashion a global system in which the world divides into ten kingdoms or districts, just as Revelation foretold.

When the world is broken up into ten administrative districts, America will still be the enforcer of stability, but Europeans may do much of the grunt work, organizing poorer regions into economic stability, much as they did during the 19th century. Europeans have been whining about having more say in the global scheme of things anyway, so this is their chance to do so.

The Bible is not clear as to how large these kingdoms will be. They could range anywhere from the size of continents to a loose collection of individual nations. Who knows, but the Scriptures indicate this will happen in the future.

Today, the United States leads the world with help from Europe. It is also naturally divided culturally and geographically into ten districts. Just as Daniel predicted, the ten toes of global governance are to be strong, but divided as they are, they are still "a mixture and will not remain united, any more than iron mixes with clay" (Daniel 2:43). I do not pretend to know the specifics of this division, but it would be quite easy to break the world up right now as follows:

Ten Potential Administrative Kingdoms (or districts)
1. North America
2. Latin America and the Caribbean
3. Sub Saharan Africa
4. North Africa and the Middle East
5. Europe
6. Russia, the Caucasus, and Central Asia
7. India and the subcontinent
8. China
9. Japan, Philippines, the Koreas, and Southeast Asia
10. Australia, New Zealand, and Oceania

There! I have saved the Europeans a great deal of trouble should they just read my book in the future. As Revelation clearly explains, the ten horns of this Western-ruled federation will not last long. Internal differences and old enemies will doom the worldwide global governance system. In addition, the power hungry antichrist will eventually topple three kings of these ten districts and bring them under his rule. In 2 Thessalonians 2:8, Paul calls this man the "lawless one," also known as the antichrist.

Scriptures in Daniel indicate that the antichrist will be of

Western/Roman descent and will therefore come from the Western world. No one knows from which country he may come, but it will definitely be a nation of Western origin. An American antichrist is not out of the question. As the antichrist takes hold over the earth, much of his power base will come from the Western world. Once Russia and the Islamic powers collapse after their ill-fated decision to invade Israel, there will be few in the world to oppose the Western dictator.

A divided yet powerful Western world today will eventually turn into an even more powerful and united world in the future. Using the combined military and economic resources of the United States and Europe, the antichrist will bring most of the world under the heel of the worst dictatorship in history.

Chapter Ten

THE ARAB WORLD: AGAINST EVERY MAN

He will be a wild donkey of a man; his hand will be against everyone and everyone's hand against him, and he will live in hostility toward all his brothers. (Genesis 16:12)

The merchants of Sheba and Dedan mentioned in Ezekiel oppose the future Russian invasion of Israel, perhaps out of fear, but also out of contempt for large outside powers. The Arabs have never been ones to fully cooperate with outside powers, and the Russian invasion will be no exception. Most, if not all, Arabic states will stay out of it, neither for nor against the invaders.

The birth of the Arabic nation is a classic bedtime story for children of all ages. In the book of Genesis, Abraham and Sarah doubted God's ability to bless Sarah with a child. She was almost eighty years old and certainly beyond childbearing age. Unwisely, the married couple decided to take matters into their own hands by forcing Hagar, an Egyptian servant of Sarah's, to have sex with Abraham until she became pregnant.

Surprisingly, Sarah became jealous of the pregnant Hagar. "You mean a married woman would be jealous of another, younger woman having sex with her husband?" you might sarcastically ask. Together Sarah and Abraham thought it would be best if Hagar and her new son disappeared into the wilderness. So began the ancient Arab/Israeli rivalry.

The angel of the LORD found Hagar near a spring in the desert; it was the spring that is beside the road to Shur. And he said, "Hagar, slave of Sarai, where have you come from, and where are you going?" "I'm running away from my mistress Sarai," she answered. Then the angel of the LORD told her, "Go back to your mistress and submit to her." The angel added, "I will increase your descendants so much that they will be too numerous to count." "The angel of the LORD also said to her: You are now pregnant and you will give birth to a son. You shall name him Ishmael, for the LORD has heard of your misery. He will be a wild donkey of a man; his hand will be against everyone and everyone's hand against him, and he will live in hostility toward all his brothers. (Genesis 16:8–12)

In this passage, God gave Hagar two significant predictions. First, he promised the descendants of Ishmael would be "too numerous to count." There are over 300 million Arabs in the Middle East, not to mentions hundreds of thousands living in other areas of the world. Unlike Western birthrates, Arabic birthrates are holding steady.

Second, God gave another apt prediction: "His hand will be against everyone, and everyone's hand against him, and he will live in hostility toward all his brothers." The history of the Arabic peoples has been one wild conflict after another. In addition to hospitality, tradition, and honor, Arabic culture has also been synonymous with war and conflict.

Their hostility towards other peoples may be a key component in their disdain for the invading powers in Ezekiel. Moreover, God explained that "he will live in hostility toward all his brothers." Not only have they been aggressive towards other peoples but also towards each other. Living in large, nomadic communities in the deserts of Arabia, it was difficult for Arabs to unite into large empires or kingdoms, at least until the rise of Mohammad.

In the next chapter of Genesis, God gave the descendants of Ishmael a lighter prophecy:

And as for Ishmael, I have heard you: I will surely bless him; I will make him fruitful and will greatly increase his numbers. He will be the father of twelve rulers, and I will make him into a great nation. (Genesis 17:20)

The "twelve rulers" were in fact twelve sons of Ishmael, and they spread their influence across the Arabian Peninsula. Today, Middle Eastern oil has made their descendants some of the wealthiest in the world.

The United Arab Emirates, Kuwait, and Qatar have some of the highest GDP per capita in the world, while the Saudi nobility is even wealthier than the Gulf Sheiks.

A History of Violence

Throughout history, the aggressive nature of the Arab peoples has made the Middle East a volatile place. In the 7th century after the birth of Christ, Arab armies stormed out of the Arabian Peninsula under the leadership of Mohammad. Mohammad, a merchant from the far western edges of the Arabian deserts, founded what has become the world's second largest religion. Quickly gaining converts, Mohammad acquired by conquest the cities of Mecca and Medina.

As a monotheist himself, Mohammad gave other monotheistic peoples a chance to convert or else become second-class citizens. Most of the Arabian Peninsula consisted of Christians, Jews, and pagan idol worshipers. Idol worshippers and nominal, lackluster Christians quickly converted to the new religion, while the most stalwart Christians and Jews fought, fled, or succumbed to being oppressed minorities.

For the next three centuries, Mohammad's descendants, known as Muslims, stormed across North Africa, Mesopotamia, and even into India and parts of China. For once, the Arabs were united under a Muslim caliphate, stretching from the Pyrenees Mountains of Spain to the jungles of Bangladesh. Entire races of people converted to Islam during this time—Egyptians, Persians, Turks, Albanians, and Moors, to name a few.

Muslim Moorish armies crossed into Europe, marching deep into France in 732 AD. For the first time in their conquests, however, the invincible Muslim armies were defeated on the battlefield of Tours. Charles Martel, also known as "The Hammer," managed to use terrain, armor, and sly tactics to send the invading armies back into Spain.

Despite their inability to conquer Europe, the Arab war machine had already accomplished tremendous feats. Moreover, Arab culture and language dominated the Middle East and North Africa. The Quran, originally written in Arabic, forced newly converted peoples to learn to both speak and read the language.

Despite their success, the ancient prophecy in Genesis began to take shape. Arabs could not maintain their empire or stay united. The first division resulted in the two branches of Islam today—Sunni and Shia. Arguments over who should succeed Mohammad soon turned to bloodshed. Sunni and Shia armies clashed with one another time and again.

Meanwhile, Turkish, Egyptian, and Persian cultures began to steal the limelight from the Arabs, and they never looked back. The Turks and Persians created lasting dynasties that would not only eclipse the Arab caliphate but also conquer large chunks of it as well. Soon, ancient Arab strongholds like Baghdad, Damascus, and Mecca became regional capitals of Ottoman and Persian Empires.

The Arabs would not gain their independence until after the fall of the Ottoman Empire in 1918. Even then, it was at the guidance of colonial Western powers, particularly France and Great Britain.

After World War II, major Arab kingdoms and nations began to formalize. Still, their hands were against every man—especially their Semitic cousins, the Jews. Four major wars were fought between the Jews and Arabs over Israel's right to exist as a nation.

In 1948, 1956, 1967, and 1973, Israel's neighbors continually sought to overthrow the new Jewish state. At times, the wars threatened to envelope the world in a nuclear holocaust by pulling the United States and the Soviet Union into the fray. Today, Palestinian suicide bombers keep Israel on edge, and they seek to bring the wrath of outside powers down upon the Israeli government. Muslim Arabs in many countries are still divided, aggressive, and angry. God's words in Genesis about the Arab people have continued to serve as a reminder of the power of prophecy. Angry Muslim Arabs, having never read the Bible, let alone read prophetic passages, continue unwittingly to fulfill prophecy. God's Word is never wrong.

What about their future role in Ezekiel's prophecy? Are Arab nations ready for a massive foreign invasion into their territory? A deeper look into five key Arab nations and peoples will determine their involvement in the prophecies.

EGYPTIANS

If there was one nation amongst the Arab peoples to call the leader, it is Egypt. Having an ancient history of their own, Egypt is only partially Arab; but they adopted Arab as their official language, and ninety percent of their people worship Allah. Egypt is also the most populated Arab nation, with over eighty million people.

Egypt played a large role in the book of Daniel as the "king of the South," referring to the Ptolemaic Dynasty. Egypt waged a continual turf war with Syria, the "king of the North," during the 3rd and 2nd centuries BC until Rome stepped in as an outside stabilizer.

The absence of Egypt from Ezekiel's prophecy indicates that Egypt will not be a part of the invasion, nor will it stand up against the invaders. There are elements in Egypt today that could play a significant role in the coming invasion. Again, neither Egypt nor the Muslim Brotherhood were mentioned in Ezekiel's prophecy, therefore making this section purely conjecture. An invasion of Israel (Egypt's neighbor) by an outside power must warrant some sort of response from Egypt. That response could be positive or negative, depending on how the Egyptian people handle the rising Muslim Brotherhood. The Muslim Brotherhood gained unprecedented power with the recent election of president Mohamed Morsi, a prominent leader of the radical group.

The Muslim Brotherhood, much like many other radicalized groups across the Muslim world, derives its roots from Sunni Wahhabi teachings. Wahhabi Sunni Islam has a much stricter outlook on the world, and has become quite popular once again in Egypt.

The Muslim Brotherhood, founded in 1928 by Sheikh Al-Banna, sought to combine modernity with traditional Islam.[1] The organization soon became a violent organization, seeking to overthrow the secular westernized Egyptian government. Egyptian President Nasser was forced to exile the radical group in 1953.[2]

This was not the end of the Brotherhood, for Egyptian migrant workers returning from Saudi Arabia in the 1970s were said to have brought the radical form of Islam back to Egypt targeting the poor, the middle class, and the religiously conservative of Egypt.[3] Again, the Muslim Brotherhood showed their true colors when they assassinated Egyptian President Anwar Sadat in 1981 for signing a peace treaty with Israel.

Hosni Mubarak succeeded Sadat and swiftly outlawed the group once again, declaring Egypt under martial law for thirty years until his own departure in 2011. Despite their second exile, however, the Muslim Brotherhood kept quite busy. Robin Wright, author of *Dreams and Shadows,* called the Muslim Brotherhood the most energized political force in Egypt.[4]

Although the Brotherhood had gone underground, they solidified their relationships with Hamas in Palestine, as well as with the opposition party against Syrian dictator Bahar al-Assad. Their influence also intensified in Egypt during the 1990s. For instance, that same decade saw the percentage of Egyptian women wearing veils increase by sixty-five percent, and the number of mosques grew substantially as well.[5]

The Muslim Brotherhood was instrumental in the 2010 revolution in Egypt, forcing Mubarak to step down from power after thirty years. After having gained a considerable number of seats in the Egyptian parliament in 2011 and the presidency in 2012, the Muslim Brotherhood became a potent political force once again. Unfortunately, their hatred for Israel runs deep.

Despite Mubarak's authoritarian style, he was at least a neutral figure towards Israel, understanding their interdependent relationship. Mubarak forbade incursions into the Gaza Strip from the Sinai Peninsula and covertly supported the economic relationship between Israel and Egypt. Since Mubarak was ousted, the Muslim Brotherhood has been increasingly vocal in their outright opposition to Israel's existence. It will be interesting in the coming years to watch President Mosni handle the pressure from his own political party to act against Israel.

Since their new rise to power, the Brotherhood has staged massive rallies in which tens of thousands chant in unison "down with Israel." In 2008, the Brotherhood managed to bring 50,000 supporters to an anti-Israel rally.[6] The Coptic Christians of Egypt have fared no better. Fear of Mubarak kept all but the most zealous anti-Christian mobs from oppressing the Christians. Not anymore. Persecutions have increased tenfold on the minority Christians.

For now, the Egyptian military still holds much power within the country. Its generals, largely secular throwbacks from the Mubarak era, have little desire to start a war with Israel. They have already fought four wars and lost. As indicated in previous chapters, Egypt cannot defeat Israel alone, and the Egyptian economy would suffer tremendously.

This is not to say that thousands of Muslim Brotherhood radicals won't seize the chance to join up with any future invaders of Israel. Should Turkey spread the word that an Islamic caliphate may be restored with the destruction of Israel, countless Muslim Brotherhood members would join the doomed invasion.

SYRIANS

A second Arab nation to keep an eye on is Syria. Both Syria and Egypt were pillars of the Christian faith in the centuries before the advent of Islam. Unfortunately, many of these Arabs disregarded their faith in Christ for Islam. In the years after Mohammad conquered the region, Syria became a pawn of various outside powers.

Passed around from Crusaders and Turks, to British and French, the Syrians have only ruled themselves independently since the 1950s. Syria has even become a pawn of yet another power today—Iran. The primary reason for Syria's closeness to Iran is that President Assad and his ruling followers are minority Alawite Shiites.[7]

Syria, always distrustful of Egypt, has looked to the Iranians as a stronger ally. In addition, relations with Turkey have improved over the past decade. Despite Sunni Turkey's disdain for the Shiite Assad regime, the two countries may continue to grow closer. Although Turkey would like to see different leadership in Syria, it will not abandon its influence in the neighboring Sunni nation. To do so would leave Syria firmly in the grip of Iran.

Regardless of the complex relationship between Syria, Turkey, and Iran, Ezekiel predicted, the Iranians, Turks, and Russians will use the Syrian gateway to Israel for their invasion. One way or another, Syria will be forced to let that massive army through the gates. It is up to the Syrians as to whether they allow the passage willingly or not. My guess is that Syria will happily open the gates. Secular or Islamic, both types of Syrians despise Israel.

Assad and his socialist/liberal pals are no friends to Israel. Still bitter about losing the Golan Heights during the 1967 War, the Syrian leader has never signed a peace treaty with Israel. Besides, with friends like Iran how could they be expected to treat Israel with respect? There are some Jews who still live in Syria, but they are required by law to carry a red card, displaying their ethnicity to police whenever they are questioned.[8] No one with a Jewish passport is allowed to enter Syria, but that is also the case in a number of other Middle Eastern nations.

In an attempt to deflect international attention from his brutal suppression of protestors in 2011, Assad paid anti-Israeli protestors to storm the borders of the Golan Heights. To an extent it worked, as media outlets zeroed in on protestors who had been shot trying to cross into Israel.

Despite Assad's brutal tactics, and significant military aid from Russia, the future leadership of Syria is in question. The secularists may be driven out by the current uprisings only to be replaced by Islamists. Syria today, unlike Saudi Arabia or Iran, is largely secular, much like Libya and Iraq.[9] Despite Syria's secular past, many Syrians have been influenced by the Muslim Brotherhood.[10] In 2010, Assad's largest opposition party was the Muslim Brotherhood.[11] Again, the goal of the Muslim Brotherhood in Syria is to bring about a Sharia caliphate across the Middle East.

The Syrian government has been under siege. Much like in the Egyptian revolution, thousands of Syrians have protested against the Alawite regime and demanded that Assad step down. According to the UN, the death toll of protestors has reached well over 7,000 and continues to climb. Islamists with the Muslim Brotherhood are not alone in their protests against Assad. Syrians desiring a chance with democracy are clamoring for his departure as well.

Democratic voices are either drowned out by Assad's gunfire, or by the Brotherhood's microphones. The two real forces vying for power in Syria are the authoritarian socialist Alawites, currently in power, and the radical Muslim Brotherhood, who would like to be in power. Either way, both groups would be more than happy to cooperate with an invading army headed for Jerusalem.

Who knows, perhaps the Russian's "anti-terror" troops under Putin's directions may decide to stay in Syria for the long haul just as they did in Afghanistan. Syria's future remains cloudy, but one thing is for sure; Syria will be involved in an Israeli invasion.

THE PALESTINIANS

The Palestinians, although not technically a nation, may undoubtedly play a role in the coming northern coalition invasion. In fact, their desire for statehood may ultimately give outside powers an excuse to invade the Jewish State.

When Jews began moving into Palestine in the late 19th century, the land had belonged to the Ottoman Empire. At the time, there were only a small, scattered number of Arabs in the region. After WWI, however, the powerful Hashemite monarchs were given Iraq and the Trans-Jordan for their faithful service against the Ottomans.[12] Palestine was considered a small part of Trans-Jordan. Arabs living along the West Bank and in Palestine may have called themselves Palestinians, but they were technically under the rule of the Jordanian Hashemite kingdom.

During the years after the fall of the Ottoman Empire, more Jews began migrating to Israel. Arabs from the surrounding countries were also drawn to Israel for jobs and food. When Jewish farmers from Europe came to the Holy Land, they brought with them the latest agricultural technologies, maximizing the potential of the Israeli countryside. By 1948, there were over a million Arabs living alongside 1.3 million Jews.[13]

In spite of the hardships, Jewish immigration to Israel skyrocketed during the decades after the Holocaust, giving the Jews a three to one edge on the Arabs already living in Israel. Jews maintained a dominant majority until the 1967 War. After Israel's defeat of Syria, Egypt, and Jordan, the Jews became the rulers of hundreds of thousands of additional Arabs in the Gaza Strip and West Bank. It was after 1967 that the Palestinians really began the cry and hue for a nation. Rallying around a charismatic ex-Muslim Brotherhood Egyptian operative by the name of Yasser Arafat, the Palestinian Liberation Organization (PLO) began a thirty-year reign of terror. Employing suicide bombers, rocket attacks, and organizing intifadas, the Palestinian group became one of the most renowned terrorist organizations in the world.

Their goals were simple—destroy the Jewish state in Palestine and set up a Palestinian nation in Gaza and the West Bank. The PLO's tactics were unsuccessful as Westerners did not take kindly to seeing small children blown up at Israeli bus stops or Jewish athletes kidnapped from Olympic games and then shot. Arafat began to try a different tact in the 1990s. By dropping the terrorist image, Arafat sought to legitimize the Palestinian's cause by exploiting the "plight" of Palestinian refugees and pinning much of the blame on the Israeli army. By pretending not to be a terrorist, he gained the Nobel Peace Prize.

The Israeli blame-game is also popular amongst the far left in America and Europe. Seeing the Palestinians as an underdog, liberal groups across the Western world sympathize with them. This is evidenced most recently in President Obama's continued demands that Israel create a Palestinian state within Israel's borders.

Israeli Prime Minister Netanyahu has made it plainly clear that he will allow the Palestinians their own nation with a few conditions—the Palestinians must allow a continued Israeli military presence, and accept Israel's right to exist as a nation. The Palestinians have balked, not just at the first condition, but also at the second. For seventy years, Palestinian leadership has refused to acknowledge Israel's right to exist. Imagine a conflict with your neighbor over the layout of the backyard fence. Not only does your neighbor believe the fence should be moved to his advantage, but he even questions whether or not your house actually belongs to you.

The Palestinians have been cursed with terrible leadership. Fatah has recently aligned itself with the radical group Hamas, another offshoot of the Muslim Brotherhood. Neither Fatah nor Hamas will recognize the Jewish nation's existence.

Knowing that their "all-Jews-should-leave-Israel-or-be-killed" argument will not hold up amongst most world leaders, the Palestinians have sought legitimacy amongst the UN and other anti-American entities. Should the UN mandate to make Palestine a nation build steam, it could also put the Israelis in a serious bind.

Outside powers, including elements of the American and European left, the UN, China, Russia, and especially Iran and Turkey, would pressure the Israelis to recognize the Palestinians. Even President Obama has pressured the Israelis to seek conciliation with the Palestinians by forcibly removing all Jews—civilian and military—from East Jerusalem and the West Bank.

Unable to comply with these demands, the Israelis are seen as "occupiers" not only by the Palestinians but also by many others in the world. Despite the unfairness of it all, world leaders will continue to condemn Israel for being "occupiers" of a foreign country—Palestine.

Should the Israelis refuse to leave the newly mandated Palestinian nation, trouble could present itself quickly. The UN, feeling pressure from Islamic nations, may seek to send a "peacekeeping force" into Israel to "remove the Israeli presence from Palestinian territory."

The UN may first seek the help of US forces, but given the history between Israel and the United States, America will decline the offer to invade Israel. The Russians, however, will gladly take up the call to restore "peace" to Palestine.

By themselves, the Palestinians have never presented a significant threat to Israel. Their new push for statehood could bring the attention of outside powers onto the tiny Jewish nation. Russians, Iranians, Turks, and potentially a slew of other UN mandated "peacekeepers" would be only too happy to invade Israel.

Again, the UN and their peacekeeping missions were never prophesied in Scriptures, but this does not negate the possibility that a UN peacekeeping mission could be the guise under which an invasion would take place.

THE SAUDIS

As the descendants of the merchants of Sheba and Dedan, the Saudis and other citizens of the Gulf States will be opposed to the invasion of

Israel. Of all the Arab states, Saudi Arabia has the most to lose from a Russian takeover. Ezekiel specifically states that it is the "plunder" that Gulf Arabs will question. Why come to the Middle East other than to plunder, not only Israel, but also the surrounding oilfields of Saudi Arabia and the Gulf States?

Saudi Arabia has been blessed by God with immense wealth. The largest oil reserves in the world reside under its sands. Its cities now mirror western ones in size and scope. Although the wealth is concentrated in the hands of the few, those few are some of the wealthiest in the world. Because of this wealth, the Saudis have made many countries jealous.

As America's number one oil provider, Saudi Arabia has had the protection of the United States for the past eighty years. In return for the expansive amount of oil sold by the Saudis, America has turned a blind eye to the treatment of the Saudi people at the hands of their own monarchy. Saudi Arabia is a classic absolute monarchy. The Saudi's have ruled Saudi Arabia since WWI without any deviation from authoritarian rule.

As the protectors of Islam's holiest cities, Saudi Arabia has had a cushion from outside invaders. Fearing the wrath of the Muslim world should any harm befall the holy cities, non-Muslim powers, including Russia, have strayed from assaulting Saudi Arabia.

As the northern coalition invades the mountains of Israel in future years, however, the Saudis will see themselves as next in line for invasion, and their protected status will be over. The deterioration of their protection has already begun. The temporary fall of Iraq, the rise of Iran, and the strained relations with the United States have chipped away at the Saudi's tenuous position in the Middle East.

Saddam Hussein frightened the Saudi monarchy, but not nearly as much as Iran has. Iraq had always been a buffer zone between the Iranians and the Arabian oilfields. Should Iranian armies seek Saudi oil, geographically, they must first go through Iraq. This fear had been unwarranted with Saddam in power, and later, the United States's presence in Iraq kept oil-hungry Iran out of Saudi Arabia.

Saddam was a terrible evil in the eyes of the Saudis, and one they even fought against in 1990 during Operation Desert Storm. Despite their misgivings about the man, he was an Arab Sunni dictator, not a Persian Shiite theocrat. Should the Americans abandon Iraq prematurely, the Saudis may have a strategic nightmare on their hands. The Saudis would be forced to become the first line of defense against Iran, and this they cannot do for lack of military capability. Moreover, Iranian incursions into Bahrain in recent years have also frightened the Saudi kingdom.

In addition, Saudi Arabia's special status with the United States has deteriorated over the years. Although America would never allow Iran to invade Saudi Arabia, the strain of 9/11, radical Islam, and the Saudi's abhorrence towards democracy has given American officials cause to question the United States's protection of the Saudi regime.

Fifteen out of the nineteen hijackers on 9/11 were of Saudi origin. Al Qaeda originated in Saudi Arabia, financed and organized by a Saudi prince named Osama bin Laden. In 2011, the Saudis quelled demonstrations for democracy in their country, although its citizens simply desired a voice in their government. Women's rights are all but invisible. Despite Saudi Arabia's issues, the status quo is much better than the potential chaos that would follow the Saudi monarch's departure.

When the future Russian invasion comes, the Saudis will not only fear being the next target but will also resent the fact that Turkey and Iran would be given control of Jerusalem. As the primary protector of Mecca and Medina, Saudi Arabia's standing in the Muslim world was enhanced. Should Jerusalem fall to the Sunni Turks, or even worse the Shiite Persians, Saudi clout would continue to deteriorate.

JORDANIANS

Nobody expects much out of Jordan these days. One of the few Arab nations with a population smaller than Israel, a hair under six million, Jordan is not a significant threat to Israel's security. Jordan is also one of the poorest nations in the Middle East, a difficult feat within itself. Nevertheless, God has a unique set of plans for the little Arab nation.

Ezekiel does not mention the land of Jordan in the Gog and Magog prophecy, but Jordan is discussed at length in Daniel, Jeremiah, and Revelation. The tiny nation of Jordan was not always called such. The

Ottomans and the British referred to the land as Trans-Jordan. Before the Romans conquered it in the 1st century BC, it was known as Nabatea. In Biblical times, three well-known groups lived in Jordan: Moabites, Ammonites, and Edomites, all of which hated the Jews.

During the antichrist's future invasion of the Middle East, described in detail in Daniel Chapter 9, the geographical nation of Jordan miraculously escapes the antichrist's grasp.

> At the time of the end the king of the South will engage him in battle, and the king of the North will storm out against him with chariots and cavalry and a great fleet of ships. He will invade many countries and sweep through them like a flood. He will also invade the Beautiful Land. Many countries will fall, but Edom, Moab and the leaders of Ammon will be delivered from his hand. He will extend his power over many countries; Egypt will not escape. He will gain control of the treasures of gold and silver and all the riches of Egypt, with the Libyans and Cushites in submission. (Daniel 11:40–43)

Although Egypt, Israel, Syria, and large parts of Africa will be conquered, the mighty Jordanians will fight off the antichrist? Only a miracle would allow such an event to occur. Why does God give Jordan such protection during this time? According to Dr. Fruchtenbaum, the answers lie in the ancient city of Petra, found in the deserts of southern Jordan.

Christians have long believed the ancient rock city, immortalized in *Indiana Jones and the Last Crusade,* would be a haven for fleeing Christians and Jews during the Tribulation, but Petra's role in Revelation is more than just a theory. Dr. Fruchtenbaum believes God gave readers three clues as to where Jews would hide from the antichrist during the last 3.5 years of the Tribulation.

In Matthew 24:16, Jesus tells Jews living in nearby Israel to "flee unto the mountains" when the abomination of desolation occurs. The nearest mountains and isolated wilderness to which the Jews could flee would be southern Jordan, namely in the areas surrounding Petra.[14] Dr.

Fruchtenbaum continues by explaining that another clue can be found in Isaiah 33:16, a passage regarding the protection of God's remnant of believers during the Tribulation: "He shall dwell on high; His place of defense shall be the munitions of rocks; His bread shall be given him; His waters shall be sure" (American Standard Version). The passage details that this hiding place is also quite defensible by being in the "munitions of rocks."[15]

Dr. Fruchtenbaum believes that a last and most obvious clue can be found in Micah 2:12:

> I will surely assemble, O Jacob, all of you; I will surely gather the remnant of Israel; I will put them together as the sheep of Bozrah, as a flock in the midst of their pasture; they shall make great noise by reason of the multitude of men. (ASV)

Today, Bozrah is the region surrounding the ruins of ancient Petra in southern Jordan. Petra is surrounded by cliffs and mountains, and its narrow mountain passes are only accessible to a few individuals at a time.[16] In *The Last Crusade,* the Nazis had to leave behind the bulk of their forces, including their tanks to follow Indy and his crew down into the city of Petra. So too will the antichrist's vast armies be handicapped by the terrain surrounding Petra.

Despite any current rage the average Jordanian Arab has towards Israel, some Tribulation Jordanians may even help the Jews escape the antichrist by hiding them in the endless caves and caverns of ancient Petra. By God's intervention, tiny Jordan will be one of the few places on earth the antichrist does not control during the Tribulation. Jews will flock there by the "multitudes."

THE REAL ARAB SPRING

As the Bible indicates, most, if not all, Arab nations will abstain from invading Israel. Despite the ancient Isaac/Ishmael rivalry, the Arabs will choose not to help the invaders. God may be intervening on Abraham's behalf to protect his ancient promise of blessing Abraham's descendants.

Perhaps in the eyes of the Arab world, the invading powers represent a far worse future than the status quo.

Although the Muslim Brotherhood may entice many to join the invaders, the Egyptian government will hopefully abstain because of its interdependence with Israel. Syria may have little choice in the matter, and the Saudis will be scared spitless. At best, an invasion of Israel would bring a new, more sinister power into the Middle East and increase the power of the Turks and Persians. At worst, the invaders would turn their eyes upon the oil-rich Arab lands surrounding Israel and seize the entire Middle East.

By abstaining from the invasion, the Arabs escape the wrath of God that is poured down upon both the invaders and their homelands. Arabs may also pick up the pieces in the Middle East, taking over lands and oil fields left behind by the ruined invaders. Ezekiel predicts that the Israelis as well will plunder the lands of its attackers for seven years after the invasion.

> Then those who live in the towns of Israel will go out and use the weapons for fuel and burn them up—the small and large shields, the bows and arrows, the war clubs and spears. For seven years they will use them for fuel. [10] They will not need to gather wood from the fields or cut it from the forests, because they will use the weapons for fuel. And they will plunder those who plundered them and loot those who looted them, declares the Sovereign LORD. (Ezekiel 39:9–10 NIV)

Moreover, nearby Arab nations will prosper significantly without the existence of Turkey and Iran in the region. The books of Jeremiah and Revelation prophecy that one Arab nation in particular will become more prosperous than all the rest. Out of the ashes of the failed Russian invasion, Babylon will arise once more.

Chapter Eleven

IRAQ AND THE NEW BABYLON

"So desert creatures and hyenas will live there, and there the owl will dwell. It will never again be inhabited or lived in from generation to generation. As I overthrew Sodom and Gomorrah along with their neighboring towns," declares the LORD, "so no one will live there; no people will dwell in it. (Jeremiah 50:39–40)

B abylon has been destroyed just as God said it would, never to be rebuilt again. At least that is a common misperception today. Many Christians point to the ruins of Babylon as evidence of God's prophecy. Unfortunately, they have been misinterpreting the prophecies, and misreading the history books. Babylon has been abandoned but never utterly destroyed by fire.

Sensationalists, looking to the latest headlines, lack a healthy respect for the literal fulfillment of Scripture, and give cities like Rome, Jerusalem, New York City, and even San Francisco the title of Babylon. Although compared to Babylon in Scripture, Jerusalem and Rome could not be the actual city of Babylon. New York City is the economic capital of the world today, but once the antichrist moves his own capital to the deserts of Iraq, America's status as an economic kingpin may be in trouble.

By the time the antichrist establishes Babylon as his capital, the Tribulation will be well underway. According to Dr. Fruchtenbaum, the establishment of Babylon as the political/economic capital of the world coincides with the last 3.5 years of the Tribulation.[1] During this time, all hell will have literally broken loose on the planet. Christians will be hunted down by the antichrist's armies, and natural disasters and plagues will be wreaking havoc elsewhere. By this point in the future, America's status as the stabilizer will be meaningless; thus losing its economic power will be the least of America's worries.

Students of history know that claims of Babylon's past destruction are just plain silly. Babylon has been conquered, abandoned, and rebuilt time and again. Never has the conflagration described in the Bible befallen Babylon. A number of prophecies regarding Babylon have yet to take place. Take the words of Isaiah for instance:

> And Babylon, the glory of kingdoms, the splendor and pomp of the Chaldeans, will be like Sodom and Gomorrah when God overthrew them. It will never be inhabited or lived in for all generations; no Arab will pitch his tent there; no shepherds will make their flocks lie down there. But wild animals will lie down there, and their houses will be full of howling creatures; there ostriches will dwell, and there wild goats will dance. Hyenas will cry in its towers, and jackals in the pleasant palaces; its time is close at hand and its days will not be prolonged. (Isaiah 13:19–22 ESV)

Isaiah predicted a number of events that will happen to Babylon which have never happened. First, Babylon has never been destroyed in a fiery blaze like Sodom and Gomorrah. A similar account of Babylon's future can be found in Jeremiah 50:39-40. From the tower of Babel to the Hanging Gardens of Nebuchadnezzer and from Alexander the Great's conquests to Saddam Hussein's regime, Babylon has been the home and cultural center of many peoples, spanning thousands of years.

Secondly, Arabs pitch their tents in the ruins of Babylon all of the time; they are known as the Iraqis. In fact, there are towns very close to the ruins of ancient Babylon. Babylon is only a mere fifty miles from Baghdad.

The third prophecy of Isaiah's passage is stranger than the rest. References to goats, hyenas, and ostriches are not meant to represent literal wild animals but rather wild demons that will haunt the old strongholds of the ancient city of Babylon. No human would dare seek shelter in the ruins of Babylon with creepers like that running around.

Babylonian History

Throughout most of history, Babylon has been inhabited. Babylon was the ancient home of Nimrod and the tower of Babel. Nimrod's plan to unite the world under his rule and against God's was not meant to be, as God dispersed mankind by confounding their languages.

From Hammurabi's Codes to Nebuchadnezzar's Hanging Gardens, Babylon continued to be a dominating presence in the ancient world. Famous for their idol worship and astrology, the Babylonians were deep into witchcraft and ungodly pursuits.

As prophesied in Isaiah, Babylon was conquered by the Medes and the Persians but never destroyed by fire, earthquake, or marauding armies. The Persians used Babylon as another capital city for their empire, one more centralized than their Persian capital at Susa.

Alexander the Great continued to use Babylon as the capital of his own short-lived empire until he too passed away. Eventually, Babylon slowly fell apart from abandonment and disarray. According to Revelation, however, it will be rebuilt again.

According to Chapter 17 of Revelation, Babylon will one day become the spiritual capital of a "one-world-super-church," devoid of God yet harnessing the power of institutional religion.[2]

> Then the angel carried me away in the Spirit into a wilderness. There I saw a woman sitting on a scarlet beast that was covered with blasphemous names and had seven heads and ten horns. [4] The woman was dressed in purple and scarlet, and was glittering with gold, precious stones and pearls. She held a golden cup in her hand, filled with abominable things and the filth of her adulteries. [5] The name written on her forehead was a mystery: BABYLON THE GREAT THE MOTHER OF PROSTITUTES AND OF THE ABOMINATIONS OF THE EARTH. I saw that the woman was drunk with the blood of God's holy people, the blood of those who bore testimony to Jesus. When I saw her, I was greatly astonished. (Revelation 17:3–6)

John describes Babylon as "Mother of the Prostitutes and of the Abominations of the earth," a reference to religious apostasy. Because she sits atop the beast with "seven heads and ten horns," she has the help of earthly governments to carry out her brutal persecution of God's people during the Tribulation.[3]

According to Revelation, not only will Babylon become a spiritual capital of the world, but it will also become an economic and political one as well. The antichrist will use and abuse the false religious institution of Babylon by destroying whatever religious system is in place in the world. He will then force everyone to worship him from his new capital.

Chapter 18 of Revelation indicates that the antichrist's political/economic world capital will burst into flames and be destroyed not long after his ascension to power, much like Sodom and Gomorrah were destroyed. Verse 18 indicates "she will be burned up with fire," while verse Revelation 18:9 mentions the "smoke of her burning."

Bear in mind it is quite difficult to see the prophecies of Babylon come to fruition today. Babylon may not even be rebuilt until after the Tribulation begins and the antichrist has been made known. Some Bible scholars believe the new Babylon won't even be rebuilt until after Russia tries to invade Israel. The Bible is not clear as to the when, but only the how in regards to Babylon.

THE BEGINNINGS OF FULFILLMENT TODAY

Could an ancient city in the desert be restored to prominence? Will Babylon become the economic, political, and spiritual capital of the antichrist's future world empire? The answer is yes, and the foundations have already been laid.

Strangely enough, the antichrist will not be the first person desiring to rebuild Babylon. The French General Napoleon Bonaparte sought to rebuild the ruins of the ancient city during his expedition to the Middle East in 1799. Mainly, he wanted to cut off British trade from India and to capture Egypt, but he had also made plans to travel to Mesopotamia. He even had architectural designs prepared in advance should he get the opportunity to rebuild the ancient city.

Not only did Napoleon desire domination over the earth, but he was also obsessively competitive as well—not competitive with the British, Austrians, or Prussians but with his long dead heroes Caesar and Alexander. If those men could conquer the world, why couldn't he? Napoleon sought to rebuild the ancient empires with himself as the emperor. Starting with Egypt, he was to proclaim himself pharaoh and then use his armies to travel eastward in an attempt to restore the ancient Babylonian city.

A disastrous sea battle in the Nile delta forced Napoleon to retreat to France, thus destroying his Middle Eastern dreams. Napoleon became the Emperor of most of Europe, but only for a season, since he was never able to unite the continent.

More recently, Saddam Hussein believed himself to be a direct descendant of Nebuchadnezzar. A lover of palaces (he had over a dozen of them), Saddam collected millions of dollars of the Iraqi government's revenue in plans to rebuild Babylon, its palaces, and all of the walls. The US military put an end to his dream.

Today, Iraq is closer than ever to once again becoming a prosperous nation, both militarily and economically. Despite the violence of insurgents and terrorists in Iraq, their future success has been written in prophecy.

Militarily, Iraq is not yet on its feet, but with training from the United States, Iraq could become one of the best-trained armies in the Middle East, if not the world. Joel Rosenberg believes Iraq, having sat out the Gog/Magog invasion, will be there to pick up the pieces after Iran has been destroyed.[4] There will be few hostile powers in the region, for Egypt and Israel will be the only other prosperous and powerful nations left.

Economically, Iraq already has tremendous potential. Regarding the restoration of the Iraqi economy, Iraqi Prime Minister Ayad Allawi stated in 2006, "We are restructuring the entire economy in an atmosphere of violence."[5] Imagine what they could accomplish when they finally have peace.

Saddam Hussein may have scared the Persians away, but economically, he was just a dictator. Dictatorships and authoritarian regimes rarely make money (the new Russia being an exception due to its tremendous energy reserves and its governmental monopolies). Once Iraq was turned into a free market democracy[6] in 2005, it was given a chance for freedom and wealth, one that would have never come under Saddam.

Another blundering error made by Saddam was that he scared off all the tourism. Iraq is home to dozens of ancient empires and peoples. Iraq has splendid museums and archeological sites, but Iraq was run by a madman and his criminally insane sons for thirty years. He could have rebuilt Babylon, but few would have visited.

Today, the Iraqi government is seeking to make that dream a reality once again. Known as the "Future of Babylon" project, archeologists with the World Monuments Fund sought a $700,000 grant in 2009 to begin reconstruction of key components of the ancient city.[7] Once Babylon is up and running, tourism to the Iraqi nation will skyrocket.

A third economic bluster during Saddam's reign was the inefficient use of his oilfields. There was little development in the two decades before Saddam's ousting, as only twenty-one of eighty oil fields were actually pumping oil.[8] He even tried to light his oilfields on fire during America's 2003 invasion.

Iraq has staggering energy potential. Their proven oil reserves rank second in the world behind Saudi Arabia, with 115 billion barrels of proven reserves.[9] Under the ruins and sands, there are much larger quantities lurking. Experts estimate that Iraq could eventually outstrip Saudi Arabia as the world's largest holder of reserves and could potentially stabilize the world's oil supply, calming the Middle East considerably.[10]

As the future economic capital of the world, it is no surprise that Iraq will eventually prosper. Given Iraq's geographical position in the world, it is also not surprising to see that the antichrist will choose Babylon for his capital.

In ancient times, Babylon was positioned along the waters of the Euphrates River, which ran straight into the Persian Gulf. Today, Iraq is perfectly centered to become the economic capital of the world. Iraq, unlike the United States, sits atop the ancient crossroads of the Middle East. It also resides along one of the world's most precious oil waterways—the Persian Gulf.

Iraq and the new Babylon could be chosen as an economic capital to allow eastern nations, such as China, India, and Japan, easier access to its goods. Babylon has and will be a strategic economic location.

It would be a bold statement to indicate that Iraq has fulfilled prophecy just yet, but the country has made significant progress. Ousting an authoritarian regime and promoting a free market with democracy, Iraq is on the right path for prosperity. Their potential oil future will only expand after the fall of Iran, giving Iraq the opportunity to rival Saudi Arabia in wealth. Should a democratic society emerge, the Iraqis will create much more wealth than the Saudis ever have. Recent attempts to rebuild Babylon indicate that perhaps the ancient city is ready to rise from obscurity.

Chapter Twelve

KINGS FROM THE EAST

The sixth angel poured out his bowl on the great river Euphrates, and its water was dried up to prepare the way for the kings from the East. Then I saw three impure spirits that looked like frogs; they came out of the mouth of the dragon, out of the mouth of the beast and out of the mouth of the false prophet. They are demonic spirits that perform signs, and they go out to the kings of the whole world, to gather them for the battle on the great day of God Almighty. (Revelation 16:12–14)

Who are the kings of the East? In Revelation, John describes the kings of the east as part of the antichrist's hordes who will join him in battle against Jesus Christ at Armageddon. Some Bible scholars point to evidences from other scriptural passages to find the identification of the "kings from the east." The "east," in other scriptural references, has been known to mean Babylonians, Assyrians, and Persians. In other words, they were Middle Eastern kings who were directly east of Israel. This theory may be true. Nevertheless, in Revelation Chapter 16 these "kings" may more likely be a reference to the seven remaining kings still helping the antichrist rule.

Looking at the situation in Revelation 16, the antichrist has already overtaken three of the ten kings of the earth, while the remaining seven help him rule. If the antichrist's political capital by this point is Babylon, one must assume that the Middle East was one of the regions or kingdoms that the antichrist had already personally overthrown.

In fact, Daniel Chapter 12 highlights his Middle Eastern takeover.

At the time of the end the king of the South will engage him in battle, and the king of the North will storm out against him with chariots and cavalry and a great fleet of ships. He will invade many countries and sweep through them like a flood. He will also invade the Beautiful Land. Many countries will fall, but Edom, Moab and the leaders of Ammon will be delivered from his hand. He will extend his power over many countries; Egypt will not escape. He will gain control of the treasures of gold and silver and all the riches of Egypt, with the Libyans and Cushites in submission. But reports from the east and the north will alarm him, and he will set out in a great rage to destroy and annihilate many. He will pitch his royal tents between the seas at the beautiful holy mountain. Yet he will come to his end, and no one will help him. (Daniel 11:40–45)

Some Bible scholars postulate that Daniel 11 is describing the antichrist's overthrow of three of the ten world kingdoms, the three kings being Iraq (east), Egypt (south), and Syria (north).[1] This theory, though, has its setbacks.

Judging from the evidence, the world rather than Europe or the old Roman Empire is to be split up into ten districts or kingdoms. No one knows exactly how large these kingdoms or districts will be, for how could the "king of the south" (Egypt), "king of the north" (Syria), and the "king of the east" (Iraq), represent three of the ten world rulers? Iraq, Egypt, and Syria may have a grand total of 160 million people. Granted, these are important historical countries, but that leaves 6.8 billion people, and ninety-nine percent of the remaining earth for the remaining seven kings to rule.

What we do know from the Daniel 12 passage is that by that point the antichrist has overthrown three of the ten kings, including the lands of Egypt, Syria, Israel, Ethiopia, Sudan, Somalia, Libya, Iraq, and potentially other African and Middle Eastern countries as well. It sounds like whoever controls the Middle East and Africa during the Tribulation had better find a less hazardous career.

To sum up the antichrist's conquests, he has conquered a Western region of the world, either Europe or North America, and added large parts of the Middle East and Africa, toppling the three kings who previously ruled those regions.

With this in mind, one must assume that the remaining "kings of the east" in Revelation Chapter 16 are plural, and that they still hold their power after the antichrist has taken over Mesopotamia and the Middle East. The kings of the east in Revelation cannot be Mesopotamian kings nor can they be Persian (the Persians were mainly destroyed by God in the Russian invasion).

Then who are the remaining kings of the east who will march with their massive armies across a dried up Euphrates River on their way to Armageddon? The only powers east of Iran who historically would have the ability to run large-scale kingdoms are India, Japan, and China.

INDIA

The world's largest democracy could very well be responsible for running a future world kingdom or district. Home to over one billion people, India's population is also very diverse. Although Hindu is the dominant religion, large numbers of Buddhists, Muslims, Sikhs, and Christians reside in India. Although India has a high amount of poverty, its economy is growing quite steadily.

Geographically, India is hemmed in by an ocean to the south, mountains to the north, and jungles to the east. The plains that run along India's northeast region border the Islamic nation of Pakistan—India's greatest rival. Even if India desired to expand, it would be nearly impossible, unless she wanted to go to nuclear war with Pakistan.

Before the arrival of the British East India Company, the geographic boundaries of India hampered homegrown Indian dynasties. Outside powers managed to sweep into India, taking advantage of the diverse and divided array of kingdoms and states within the subcontinent.

Aryans, Mongols, Muslims, and British managed to exploit India's fragmented nation. It was only the ancient Mauryans who managed to unite India under Indians. Nevertheless, India is once again united under Indian leaders. Due to geographic limitations, their borders are etched in stone, but their influence and sea power will grow in the coming years.

Culturally, the majority of Indians are Hindu. Seen as more pacifist in nature than Muslim or even Christian societies, India has never been one for expansion. Nevertheless, with nuclear weapons, one billion people, and a rough history with Pakistan, India could become an aggressive power if it so desired.

Despite their locked-in geographical status, India's military, economy, and leadership abilities qualify the nation as a potential "king of the east," able to influence and reign over much of South Asia.

CHINA

The ancient Chinese had a nickname for China. They called it the "Middle Kingdom," meaning the center of the earth. All affairs outside of China had little bearing on one of the world's largest countries. Throughout its history, China has been one of the most inward focused, mysterious places on earth.

China has a long history of centralized government. From Shi Huangdi, China's first emperor who united most of China under his rule, to Mao Zedong, the first Communist party leader, Chinese governments have ruled over millions of their people with absolute power.

China has consistently created, invented, and innovated its way through history. The Chinese were the first to invent paper and gunpowder. According to Marco Polo, the Chinese also invented spaghetti. Chinese goods dominated the Silk Road and they continue to dominate world markets today. One thousand years ago it was silk, but today it is cheap consumer products.

There is no doubt that China is a major economic superpower. With the world's largest consumer product sales, China has the third largest economy in the world. Since the Communist party of China has opened the door in their economic zones to capitalism, China's growth has been unmatched in the past two decades. Despite their success, as explained earlier, when eighty percent of its citizens live far below the poverty line, sustained economic growth will be hard to continue.

Because of their vast size geographically, militarily, and economically, China may very well become a "king of the east." In order to do so, China will need to make some changes. China's history with implosion and potential economic catastrophe will have to be dealt with should China rise to superpower status.

Despite their size and aggressive posturing, China is not an expansionist power. The whole purpose of calling themselves the "center of the earth" was so they would not have to worry about the rest of the world. China's history with isolationism runs deep. The Ming Dynasty of the 16th century closed its doors to the outside influences of Portugal and Spain, feeling that outside Western powers might corrupt the core of China. China spent the next 300 years isolated from the rest of the world's advances, and they have paid a price.

Being an isolationist power, China has had unfortunate troubles with outside powers. Despite its vast size, China's military has never been massive and powerful. Even today, China's military is not what it should be considering it has the world's third largest economy and the largest population. The Mongols successfully invaded China in the 11th century, and the Western powers, to an extent, invaded China in the 19th century.

During the 19th century, China was involuntarily forced to join the rest of the world thanks to Europe's colony race. European powers, such as the British, German, French, Japanese, and Dutch, alongside the Japanese and Americans, competed with one another to gain access to China's vast markets. The Opium Wars against Britain were fought primarily to keep the opium trade up and running. With European warships lurking nearby, the Chinese had little choice but to succumb to Western pressures.

China still continued to isolate itself from the world until the Japanese invaded, conquered, and subjugated much of its east coast. After WWII, Communist ideology spread through China's rural poor, enticing them with the chance of equality with the eastern merchants.

Only when the Chinese Communists under Mao Zedong came to power did China seek to broaden its horizons. Even so, China only conquered the pacifist Buddhist nation of Tibet in the 1950s. Even the tiny island nation of Taiwan has thus far managed to evade a Chinese invasion.

Geographically, China has little choice but to remain an isolated, inward-focused nation. Penned in by mountains and jungle to the south, ocean to the east, and deserts to the west, China has only one way to advance—into Mongolia and Russia.[2] A confrontation with Russia is not in the best interests of China; therefore, Chinese expansion is "dead in the water."

Demographically, most Chinese live on the coastal plain in the large cities of Hong Kong, Beijing, and Shanghai. Almost all of China's factories and infrastructure lay within one hundred miles of the coast.[3] Just as in the days of the Emperors and the Communists, the majority of the wealth is concentrated in the hands of the few, as eighty percent of China is very poor, and only five percent would be considered middle class.[4] Chinese policy makers will eventually have to deal with the masses of rural and urban poor in their midst, an issue that will plague China's growth immeasurably.

Economically, China has a great divide. Friedman explains that China's business class will have no desire to expand their markets to the poor masses because they actually have more in common with foreign investors than with their own government.[5]

A future showdown between China's businesses and foreign investors, the poor masses, and Communist government is inevitable. How China handles this potential crisis will determine what kind of power China will have in the coming years as a "king of the east."

JAPAN

Of all the Asian nations in the world today, Japan has the best opportunity to rule them all. Island nations can be surprising forces in this world, primarily because they are protected by their geography. Britain's island status protected it from numerous invasions by Vikings, Spanish, French, and Germans. Similarly, Japan was protected from a massive Mongol invasion in the 12th century.

Being an island also enables governments to consolidate their power quicker, unifying their people more easily. Both the British and the Japanese spent energy and time uniting their people under one banner, and when unification came, it was long lasting. China spent considerable time trying to unite its many cultural groups under one language, government, and currency. On the other hand, Japan had a much easier time, since there is only one dominant language and culture on the island—Japanese.

Japan will perhaps become the most powerful Asian nation again for three reasons: its history of military success, its need for expansion, and its ability to reinvent itself.

MILITARY PROWESS

The Japanese have always been a warrior culture. Legends of ninjas and samurai's battling through medieval Japan still resonate in Japanese culture today. The Japanese feudal system, similar to the European system, was every bit as warlike as their Western counterparts but lasted 300 years longer.

Japan was perhaps an even more closed society than China. When Portuguese merchants and missionaries arrived on the shores of Japan in the 15th century, the Japanese at first welcomed them. When the Shoguns began to feel threatened by Christianity, misunderstanding the promises of freedom that Christ gave to its converts, they barred any foreigners from visiting Japan.

The doors to Japan's converts and its markets stayed closed for 400 years, until American Admiral Matthew Perry showed up with his warships in 1853. Japanese leaders were given an ultimatum: open your doors to trade or continue to remain behind the times. From 1853 to 1901, Japan poured its soul into becoming a modernized power. They understood that the only way to beat the Western powers was to become like them. Employing western military experts, engineers, and architects, Japan began to recreate themselves into an industrial power. What took Europeans 400 years to do, the Japanese did in a mere fifty. Japan had gone from the Middle Ages to the modern age in less than a generation.

To gain resources and prove to the world that they were a force to be reckoned with, Japan expanded toward the largest power of all—Russia. It's the classic "go for the biggest, ugliest guy in the room" approach.

If Japan could defeat Russia in a war, who couldn't they beat? Immediately the other Western powers would be forced to respect Japan's new power.

The Russo-Japanese war was a rout from the start. With speed and surprise, Japanese warships attacked Russian ports and bested the Russian fleet repeatedly. It was so devastating for the Russians that outside powers were forced to intervene before the entire Russian military collapsed. Much like the Spanish-American War announced the arrival of America as a world power, the Russo-Japanese War cast Japan into the upper echelons of world power status.

Always looking to expand, the Empire of the Rising Sun then conquered Korea and Manchuria. By the 1930s, only one other Pacific power threatened Japanese dominance over that ocean—the United States. Both powers were expanding their naval capacities eastward and westward, and they practiced war games with the other as the target.

The inevitable clash came on December 7, 1941, as Japanese bombers surprise-attacked Pearl Harbor, thereby bringing America into World War II. Before bringing the "sleeping giant" into the fray, Japan had been quite busy conquering large sections of China as well as Southeast Asia. By 1942, Japan had created a massive Pacific Empire; it stretched from the island nations of Papua New Guinea and Indonesia to the very gates of India. Even the American-occupied Philippines were conquered by the Japanese.

Like all other opponents of the US military, the Japanese eventually succumbed to American military power. Despite their defeat in WWII, the Japanese rise to power was impressive. In a matter of fifty years, the Japanese had gone from an isolated medieval kingdom to a world power.

NEED FOR EXPANSION

What caused such a drastic change in the course of half a century? Industrial revolution in Japan spurred the need for raw resources, mainly resources Japan did not have. As an island, Japan is extremely reliant upon outside sources to feed its industry. Japan has timber and fish aplenty, but what it does not have is oil, precious metals, or iron ore.

Their lack of natural resources explains why Japan was so aggressive during the first half of the 20th century. It also explains why Japan was so jumpy about American sea power in the Pacific. Japan is literally held hostage by the maintenance of open sea-lanes.[6] Should an outside power usurp control of those lanes, Japan's status as an industrial power would evaporate overnight. Japan did all it could to strengthen its naval capabilities, but it was not enough to counter American sea power. Japan was wise enough to realize the futility of fighting the Americans. Rather than fight the United States, Japan now relies on American control of sea-lanes.[7]

JAPAN TODAY

After World War II, Japan threw all of its aggressive military past into an economic future. America helped rebuild Japan after the devastation of the atomic bombs and also protected Japan from Communist aggression.

Today, Japan has the world's second largest economy. Its technology and industrial products are nearly unmatched. From cars to stereo systems, Japanese products are top notch. Japan's success economically and its alliance with the United States has enabled it to rebuild in other avenues as well.

Despite her shrinking population and recent economic woes, Japan has managed to retain its position as a dominant regional power. Japan's navy is once again the most dominant in the Pacific World.[8] Japan is also the world's third largest nuclear power generating nation, just behind France and the United States, with forty-four nuclear reactors (forty-two after the horrendous earthquake/tsunami/nuclear meltdown in 2011).[9] Japan is a defacto nuclear nation, and it would not take much effort should Japan desire to build nuclear weapons.

As strategist Joseph Nyse Jr. explains, "Japan has an impressive ability to reinvent itself."[10] From reinventing itself from a sleepy land of fishing villages to a world power, to picking itself up again after WWII to become one of the world's dominant economies, Japan has proven itself time and time again.

In the future, Japan's need for raw resources and open sea lanes will ensure that it keeps an eye on the Middle East and world events. Unlike they were in the 15ᵗʰ century, Japan will keep both its doors and eyes open.

WE THREE KINGS

A lot could change in Asia between now and the end of the known world. No one knows for sure who the "kings of the East" will be as they march from their strongholds to fight Jesus Christ and his saints in Israel. If the end is soon, as the next few chapters will indicate, one must take these three nations into serious consideration.

Part III
SOONER THAN LATER

Chapter Thirteen

IS THE END NIGH?

Now there is in store for me the crown of righteousness, which
the Lord, the righteous Judge, will award to me on that day -
and not only to me, but also to all who have longed for his
appearing. (2 Timothy 4:8)

Christians have been eagerly awaiting Christ's return since he left,
and according to 2 Timothy 4:8, "those who longed for his appearing" will be richly rewarded. The apostolic church figured he
would return within a generation. Little did they know that at least 2,000
years of history would first take place.

Christians have always cited the declining morality of the world as
evidence of the coming apocalypse, but the world has always been full
of people who are immoral by nature. In Matthew Chapter 24, Jesus predicted the "rise of false prophets," the "increase in wickedness," and
Christian "persecution" as indicators of his approaching return. These
prophecies are no doubt coming to light today, but they are more difficult
to see since these sinful human activities have been with us since the
beginning.

Another indication that we are nearing the end times is the arrival
of Revelation's last church age—Laodicea. Most dispensational Bible
scholars see evidence of prophetic writings in the chapters of Revelation
that deal with the church. Each of the seven churches represents literal
churches in Asia Minor, but their gifts and shortfalls can be applied to
churches throughout the Church Age, including today.

Moreover, each of the seven churches represents an age of church
history. This is where Revelation's status as a book of prophecy comes
into play. Specific dates vary, but dispensational Bible scholars seem to
agree with Dr. Fruchtenbaum's categorization that the 20th and 21st centuries saw the rise of the last Church Age in Revelation: "apathy, false
doctrine, and luke-warmness."

Today, the geopolitical signs are all around us. More concrete in nature, they are easier to ascertain. From Israel's restoration to the alignments of Ezekiel's Gog/Magog invasion, God is preparing the world for the Tribulation.

Just before the Tribulation occurs, however, God will rapture his Church from danger. The Lord himself explained that the last 3.5 years of the Tribulation will be so terrible that "if those days had not been cut short, no one would survive." The Tribulation is a time of God's wrath pouring out on a sinful world. The devil is literally let loose upon the earth. Environmental and economic disasters, coupled with wars, famines, and persecutions, make the Tribulation the worst seven years in history.

The antichrist spends the last 3.5 years of it hunting down and beheading Christians. Jesus himself returns to destroy the antichrist and his armies at the Battle of Armageddon, ending the Tribulation and beginning his 1,000 year Millennial reign upon the earth.

Fortunately, God was gracious enough to give followers of Christ a get-out-of-Tribulation card with the Rapture. Those who have accepted Christ as savior will, as Paul explains in 1 Thessalonians, be raptured up with him before the Tribulation begins.

> According to the Lord's own word, we tell you that we who are still alive, who are left till the coming of the Lord, will certainly not precede those who have fallen asleep. For the Lord himself will come down from heaven, with a loud command, with the voice of the archangel and with the trumpet call of god, and the dead in Christ will rise first. After that, we who are still alive and are left will be caught up together with them in the clouds to meet the Lord in the air. And so we will be with the Lord forever. Therefore encourage each other with these words. Now, brothers, about times and dates we do not need to write to you, for you know very well that the day of the Lord will come like a thief in the night. (1 Thessalonians 4:15–5:2)

There are pessimists of every flavor, such as those who say, "People have been waiting for almost 2,000 years, and they could wait another 2,000." Way to rain on the parade. Yes, people have been waiting for some time, but just like a four-hour wait for an amusement park ride, there is an end in sight. History has been steadily building to a point in which the world will finally be ready for Christ's return.

As Paul explained, the Rapture could come at any moment. This knowledge has kept the early church vigilant and watchful, just as it should our own churches today.

Unlike the Tribulation, no one knows exactly when the Rapture will come. One thing is for sure—the Rapture will occur before the Tribulation, not in the middle or the end. The Church is not mentioned after Revelation Chapter 3 and is never mentioned in Old Testament Scripture as being present during the Tribulation.

On the other hand, the Tribulation has specific signs to indicate its beginning. Since the Tribulation occurs sometime shortly after the Rapture, Tribulation signs can also act as potential indications that the Rapture may be near as well. The Tribulation begins with one event—the antichrist's signing of a peace agreement with the nation of Israel. Daniel 9:27 says,

> He will confirm a covenant with many for one "seven." In the middle of the "seven" he will put an end to sacrifice and offering. And on a wing of the temple he will set up an abomination that causes desolation, until the end that is decreed is poured out on him.

The "he" being referred to in Daniel is the antichrist. For the first 3.5 years of the "seven," Israel will have peace with the antichrist. Then, as Daniel and Revelation indicated, the antichrist will turn his rage against Israel, ending sacrifices in Israel and hunting down God's people. The covenant with Israel is what officially begins the Tribulation. When this covenant occurs, the church will be gone, as will almost anyone who recognizes the antichrist for who he is.

Christians must recognize the times. Those who bury their heads in the sand in regards to political and global events do themselves no favors. The Jewish generation of Jesus's coming failed to read the signs of the season, and many missed out on the greatest gift of all. Jesus says of this generation:

> And He was also saying to the crowds, "When you see a cloud rising in the west, immediately you say, 'A shower is coming,' and so it turns out. "And when you see a south wind blowing, you say, 'It will be a hot day,' and it turns out that way. "You hypocrites! You know how to analyze the appearance of the earth and the sky, but why do you not analyze this present time?" (Luke 12:54—56)

Today, many in the Church fail to analyze world events around them. From previous chapters, one can see that the season is at hand. Below are the six geopolitical events that must happen before the Tribulation can take place.

SIX GEOPOLITICAL EVENTS THAT MUST TAKE PLACE BEFORE THE TRIBULATION

1. WORLD WAR I AND WORLD WAR II (1914-1918; 1939-1945)

Obviously, these calamitous geopolitical events have already taken place. Both 1914 and 1939 were prophetic years, for they began the wars of nations against nations. As mentioned in Chapter 3, these wars were prerequisites for the end. As Jesus indicated, warfare that included nations rising against nations was a sign for the coming end. In Matthew 24:7 Jesus separated these world wars from other wars, "Nation will rise against nation, and kingdom against kingdom. There will be famines and earthquakes in various places." Less obvious is the prophecy regarding famines and earthquakes, both of which have increased in the previous century.

Immediately after Jesus mentioned nations rising against nations, he went into detail regarding the Tribulation. The assumption must be made that the Tribulation could not occur without these massive wars having taken place.

Historically, WWII brought about the geopolitical climate for the next necessary end-times ingredient with the establishment of Israel in the Holy Land. World War II also solidified the West's greatest conqueror, the United States, as the leader of the Western world. In the ensuing decades, the United States has enhanced and protected the global system.

2. THE RETURN OF THE JEWISH NATION TO THE LAND OF ISRAEL (1948)

One of the least debated geopolitical prerequisites for the beginning of the Tribulation is the establishment of the nation of Israel. Discussed in Chapter 3 of this book, Israel's regathering in 1948 was the last regathering of Israel before the Millennium. How could the antichrist make a covenant with the Jewish nation of Israel to begin the Tribulation without an existing Jewish nation in Israel? Prophesied by Jesus, Jeremiah, Daniel, Isaiah, Ezekiel, and others, the regathering of Israel was a prerequisite for the Tribulation. Without the Jews ruling in Israel today, no Tribulation can take place.

3. JEWISH CONTROL OF JERUSALEM (1967)

For the antichrist to sacrifice the abomination in the Temple, two events must have already taken place—the Jews must have control of Jerusalem, and the Temple must already be built. Although the Jewish Temple has not been rebuilt, its construction would have been impossible without Jewish control of Jerusalem.

The year Israel defeated a joint Jordanian-Egyptian-Syrian invasion of the country (1967) was indeed a prophetic year. Not only did it fulfill Scripture in Isaiah, but it also gave control of East Jerusalem back to the Jews.

4. GOG AND MAGOG INVASION

"In future years," Israel is to be invaded by Magog and a number of other nations for the purposes of plunder. After the battle is won by God, Israel spends seven months burying the dead and uses the leftover weapons as fuel for the next seven years.

Then those who live in the towns of Israel will go out and use the weapons for fuel and burn them up—the small and large shields, the bows and arrows, the war clubs and spears. For seven years they will use them for fuel. (Ezekiel 39:9)

The amount of time spent using the invaders' fuel, combined with the invasion having taken place after Israel's regathering, tells readers that it cannot occur during the Tribulation. The last 3.5 years of the Tribulation will be spent running from the antichrist, not plundering, using fuel, or burying the dead. For timing purposes, this battle must occur at some point before the Tribulation.

The supernatural results of this battle will lead many people to Christ, as there will be no doubt regarding who actually wins this battle. The invasion of Israel may also set up the antichrist to take over large portions of Russia's old sphere of influence, as well as position him to sign a peace deal with Israel. Although many thousands of Jews will get saved, a larger number will not; and rather than look to God, they will sign a peace treaty with the western dictator.

Additionally, the rivalry between Russia and the West cannot take place during the Tribulation, as the antichrist will be the overwhelming political force of the time. After he conquers the Middle East and Africa, the remaining seven kings of the earth cede their power to the antichrist for the last 3.5 years of the Tribulation. The lands ruled by the seven kings will undoubtedly include the old Russian lands. Although the antichrist will experience much opposition, a large Russian opposition does not fit in geopolitically with the rest of the Tribulation.

5.   THE DIVISION OF THE WORLD INTO TEN KINGDOMS

Another pre-tribulation event that has not yet occurred is the division of the world into ten regions, or kingdoms. Led by the Western "feet of iron and clay" in Daniel, the world will eventually try their hand at global governance. The global government fails quickly (probably because it was run by the UN), and is replaced by ten global regions.

The ten kingdoms qualify as a prerequisite for the Tribulation because of the rise of the antichrist. For the antichrist to sign a pact with Israel, he must at that time be the head of at least one Western country. According to Daniel Chapter 8, the antichrist's "little horn" sprouts out of one of the ten kingdoms to conquer three of the existing kingdoms. He will not accomplish his conquests until after he signs a deal with Israel, but he does come to prominence during this divisional time. Therefore, the world must be split amongst ten kingdoms before the Tribulation.

The world is not that far off from seeking a global structure. This future global government does not need one currency, one language, and one actual government. All it needs is the participation of a majority of the world's governments in an attempt to govern the world.

Today, with America as its head, the world is nearly in a global system. There is already a dominant language, culture, and currency, but they are by no means the only ones. The United States' military forces manage to stabilize the world and the president's decisions reach far across the globe.

Other nations also play a very large role. Regional powers maintain stability by balancing each other (except for the Middle East). The world's nations are integrated and interdependent economically, even the United States. The future may see Europe take a larger role in an attempted global governance system. As Scripture indicates, however, Russia and the Middle East will be continuous thorns in the sides of the West as they seek to govern the globe.

It is only after the fall of Russia, Turkey, Iran, and various other anti-Western nations in their calamitous attack on Israel that the West can truly divide the world to their liking. This division opens the way for the antichrist.

6. THE RISE OF THE ANTICHRIST

The most obvious geopolitical event before the Tribulation is the rise of the antichrist. The antichrist will be of European descent, but he does not necessarily have to live in Europe, as nearly every continent has Europeans living in them. He must, however, come out of a Western nation, and most likely a powerful one. He could be American, French, British, Italian, or any other European brand, but he will rise to prominence via politics and/or the military. Revelation 6:2 explains that the antichrist will gain notoriety through war: "I looked, and there before me was a white horse! Its rider held a bow, and he was given a crown, and he rode out as a conqueror bent on conquest." There is more evidence of the antichrist's military path in the book of Daniel.

> He will attack the mightiest fortresses with the help of a foreign god and will greatly honor those who acknowledge him. He will make them rulers over many people and will distribute the land at a price. (Daniel 11:39)

Being heavily invested in conquest, the antichrist may come from a western nation that already has a strong reputation for war and conquest.

Another cruel aspect of the antichrist's career is the practice of beheading. Some authors and students of prophecy commonly cite these beheadings as evidence that the antichrist will be a Muslim.

> I saw thrones on which were seated those who had been given authority to judge. And I saw the souls of those who had been beheaded because of their testimony about Jesus and because of the word of God. They had not worshiped the beast or its image and had not received its mark on their foreheads or their hands. They came to life and reigned with Christ a thousand years. (Revelation 20:4)

Although it is clear that he does favor beheadings, he cannot be a Muslim for a variety of reasons. First, the book of Daniel already made it clear that he is to be ethnically Roman/Western. As most Western/European-descended nations practice Christianity (at least nominally) and are democracies, this considerably slices the antichrist's chances of being a Muslim.

Second, Daniel explains:

He will show no regard for the gods of his ancestors or for the one desired by women, nor will he regard any god, but will exalt himself above them all. (Daniel 11:37)

No self-respecting Muslim would follow a man who has denounced Allah. He would immediately be labeled an apostate and probably beheaded himself. Besides, they would think it a bit odd that the man has no desire for women. Remember, Radical Islamists do not blow themselves up for nothing. Besides waging jihad for Allah, they receive seventy virgin brides upon entering paradise.

Third, the antichrist must come from a time when the democratic Western nations rule the globe—an offshoot of the Roman Empire and the Western world. The world will not be ruled by an Islamic caliphate, but by a Western, bloated, bureaucratic nightmare. This collective body of democratic nations will be bent on governing and legislating the world to promote peace, fairness, toleration, political correctness, social justice, wealth redistribution, low carbon footprints, and safe eating habits—similar to the UN but with more power. It will be a Libertarian's worst nightmare. It is from this nightmare that the antichrist will be revealed.

During his rise to power, only Christians will have an educated guess as to the identity of the antichrist. Paul explains that the rise of the antichrist will be a sign that Christians will see just before the Rapture. Paul hints in 2 Thessalonians that the "man of lawlessness will be revealed." The only folks on earth who would know about the antichrist would be students of Scripture, but they would soon be raptured before giving much warning.

Besides, if you told someone you knew who the antichrist was, you would immediately lose credibility. Those who claim to know the antichrist in the future will be labeled insane just as those who claimed Barack Obama, George Bush, Bill Clinton, Ronald Reagan, and Madonna were the antichrists were considered unstable.

No one knows who the antichrist is today, but he may already be walking the earth, waiting for his appointed time. The earth has yet to be divided into ten kingdoms, but the world wars and Israel's reestablishment in the Holy Land have taken place. The Western world is the most dominant culture on earth, and it is only a matter of time before they seek to fashion the earth more to their liking, that is into ten kingdoms.

The Gog/Magog invasion could occur at any moment as Russia, Turkey, and Iran have aligned themselves together against Israel and the West. But demographic issues indicate that Russia had better hurry if it wants to fulfill prophecy.

WHERE HAVE ALL THE BABIES GONE?

Fear of overpopulation was the hype long before global warming and even before climate change. "Stop having so many children or we're all going to die." "Mother earth cannot take anymore." "Make love not babies." Having too many children became synonymous with not caring for the environment, or purposely starving people in Africa. China bought into the fear and forcibly halted their breeding. The one-child policy in China did more than slow Chinese birthrates—it created one of history's largest infanticides, with the deaths of untold numbers of female babies.

Today the population boom is nearing its end. By mid-century, even the most fertile nations of the world will calm down and stabilize. Long before the mid-century, the world's older, mature nation-states will experience heavy population losses. The same nations who buy into global warming fears and who bought into the overpopulation scare have spent the past thirty years under-populating their future. With immigration and a healthy respect for breeding, the United States is holding steady with a 2.1 percent national birthrate.

Europe is not so lucky. Both Western Europe and Russia are experiencing the lowest birthrates of modernized nations. Within a generation, Europe will lack the manpower to ensure their economies remain intact. Factories will lose workers, armies will lose soldiers, and hospitals will lose doctors.

What do the reproductive habits of Europeans have to do with prophecy? Such heavy losses in population of both Europe and Russia mean that the prophecies of Ezekiel, Daniel, and Revelation either have to be fulfilled quickly or wait another 500 years. Either events play out in the very near future, or the Muslims will conquer Europe, and the Russians will fade into history. It would take a very long time for both Russia and Europe to regain their power should a geopolitical catastrophe of that nature occur. Given the other geopolitical clues, my guess is sooner rather than later.

EUROPE'S ISLAMIC PROBLEM

Europeans are not breeding, but their immigrants are. Europe is experiencing high levels of immigration; namely from Islamic nations. France, Great Britain, and Germany are experiencing the highest numbers of Islamic immigrants. At the rate Europe's population is dropping, the Western continent could become largely Islamic rather than Christian, or at least nominally Christian. Should Europe one day lose its Western heritage, the prophecies of Daniel and Revelation would have to wait until Europe restores its former Western self and ousts the Muslims.

While the Western world is the legitimate heir to the Roman world, the Islamic world is not. The Western world created the global system that will eventually lead to a global governance system; Islam did not. The Western world will eventually lead those ten kingdoms; Islam will not.

Whoever the antichrist will be, his name will not be Mohammad, for the Bible is clear that the antichrist will be of Roman/Western descent. Even being of Western descent, both the antichrist and radical Islamic terrorists have an affinity for beheadings, but so did the French and the English. Both radical Muslims and the antichrist have a severe anti-Semitism problem, but so too did the Germans and the Russians.

Both progressive Europeans and traditional Muslims desire global government but in vastly different ways. Progressive Europeans want a one-world socialist utopia, complete with free public transit, free public healthcare, free food, and three months paid vacations for all. I can just hear Nancy Pelosi shouting, "These are universal rights!"

Sharia Muslims desire a worldwide caliphate with an all-Muslim government, public Koran readings, public stonings and beheadings, and universal longest beard contests.

No, Islam is not a Greco-Roman descendant destined to create a ten-kingdom global system, or spawn the antichrist. If Europe wants to get with the program, they have to accomplish one of three things: have a lot more children, isolate the growing threat of radical Islam within Europe, or plead with Christ to come back sooner rather than later. I am pulling for the last option myself.

OPTION 1: HAVE MORE BABIES.

If Europeans want to keep their culture and abstain from renaming their continent Europistan, they must have more children. Currently Europe's collective fertility rate in 2009 was 1.38.[1] A fertility rate of 2.1 is needed to slowly increase or maintain a population level.

Within forty years, Germany will lose ten percent of its population, Poland twenty percent, and Russia almost twenty-five percent.[2] France, one of the more populous European nations, is currently experiencing some of the biggest changes. Nearly ten percent of its population is now Muslim[3], and its Muslim population is predominantly young, unemployed, and angry. In fact, the only increasing birthrates in Europe come not from Europeans, but rather from Middle Eastern and North African Muslim immigrant families.

Britain is not immune to the Islamization of Europe. In 2005, sixty percent of all British Muslims desired to live under Sharia law, a feat not altogether impossible. As the Archbishop of Canterbury declared in 2008, "The introduction of Sharia law for some in the UK is inevitable."[4]

It would be a happy ending for Europe if the Muslim immigrants were like the Kenyans, Indians, or Burmese who assimilated into the new cultures. America was great at assimilating newcomers into the culture because it had so much to offer (not saying anything against Polish, Italian, Mexican, or Irish culture). Moreover, newcomers to Britain, Germany, and France should have to assimilate to succeed in their new homeland.

Assimilation is not the way with Muslim populations. According to most current political scientists, Muslim cultures do not assimilate into their new homes. Instead, they become more traditionally rooted when they are faced with adversity. Seeing Western culture as vastly different, most Muslim immigrants will seek out other Muslims in an effort to sustain their own Islamic culture.

Unlike Christianity, Buddhism, or Hinduism, Islam is a political entity in addition to being a religion. In many Muslim countries, the laws of the Koran are the laws of the land. Politicians and leaders cannot lead their nations unless they are practicing Muslims. Failure to practice Islam in an approved fashion could lead to persecution from the government itself.

The largest political component of Islam is that of jihad and the global caliphate. Many Muslims, including immigrants to Europe, see themselves on a greater mission, i.e., to spread Islam across the globe. Much like Christian missionaries of the 19th century trekked across the deserts of Africa and the Jungles of Asia, today's Muslim missionaries seek converts in the skyrises of New York and the subways of London.

A majority of Muslim immigrants refuse to assimilate into Western culture because they want to convert Western culture itself. The more violent types such as Al Qaeda seek to destroy and kill non-Muslim cultures, while the more cunning, peaceful types slowly erode the weaker cultures from the inside out, until the people have no choice but to become Islamic.

The process of Islamization is in full swing in European countries. Rather than compromise with local officials, Muslim communities are becoming increasingly confrontational in their approach. Demanding Sharia law, and failing to comply with Western laws, Muslims in Europe have become a vocal crowd indeed. Oxford, England, one of the most Christian cities of Europe, has responded to the demands of local Muslims by broadcasting the Muslim call to prayer three times daily from a local mosque.[5]

Europeans today vastly outnumber Muslim immigrants, but their majority is diminishing rapidly. If Muslim fertility rates hold steady, there could be thirty million Muslims by 2025.[6] Because of Muslim persistence in sticking together in communities and voting blocs, these numbers present a serious challenge to European governments. Should the numbers maintain their consistency, the year 2050 could see Europeans themselves outnumbered … in their own countries and on their own continent. If the prophecies of Daniel and Revelation are going to fulfill themselves in the near future, they must happen quickly before Europe is no longer Western.

Option 2: Confront Islam

Because the Scriptures have never been proven wrong, one must assume that Europe will somehow maintain its "Westernness." For Europeans to accomplish this, they must solve their immigration problems. Just as the immigration debate in the United States has become a prickly issue, so too has it become a sensitive issue in Europe.

European politicians have become painfully aware of the growing Muslim voting bloc. What European politician is going to stand up and say, "It's time for Europeans to get busy and reproduce," or "All radicalized, non-assimilating Muslims must leave the country"? Not too many, unless they enjoy being called a racist bigot by the majority of liberal progressive Europeans.

Somehow, Europe will have to confront the Islamic challenges to their Western culture. It is possible that European backlash to continued Muslim immigration will create strong political parties that will rally Europeans together. Perhaps France will enact stringent immigration laws, or Germany will make it less appealing for immigrants to come to Germany. One way or another, they must assimilate their immigrant populations or develop incentives for European families to have nine or ten children. Maybe we should send the Duggar family to England and give them some pointers!

Option 3: The Tribulation occurs sooner than expected

It may be possible for Europeans to save their continent on their own, but this is doubtful, all things considered. The best solution to this long-term problem would be the fulfillment of prophecy sooner rather than later. Should Western governments seek to usher in a global governance system now, consolidating their power with the United States and organizing the world to their liking, there would be little that current Muslim populations in Europe could do to stop them.

Moreover, should events unfold quickly enough, bringing about the Tribulation, Europe will have little to fear from long term Muslim immigration. As it stands in the next decade, Europe will still remain a solidly Western place. In fact, should the Tribulation occur soon, immigration would be the least of their worries, for they would soon find themselves ruled by a satanic dictator instead.

THE ARMIES OF RUSSIA WITHOUT SOLDIERS?

Russia is experiencing an even worse shortage of babies than Europe. It was the immense size of the Russian army that kept Napoleon at bay in 1811. In 1914, the Germans, on the brink of world war, were so afraid of the Russian hordes that they attacked Russia preemptively, hoping to slow the Russian army from mobilization. It was this same megalithic Russian army that conquered half of Europe during WWII, defeating the Nazis in the process. Americans were so afraid of the red tide of Russian communism sweeping across North America that Hollywood made movies about Russian invasions.

Today, Russia's army is no greater than other regional powers. Russia does have access to a sizeable fleet and an array of nuclear weapons, but what the Russian government does not have are enough men and women to field her armies. Russia's birthrates are the lowest of Europe, and perhaps in the world at 1.14 percent.[7] Its culture, largely secular and progressive, has little incentive or desire to procreate anymore. As mentioned previously, Russia's abortion rates are sky high, and not even the great Putin can convince Russians to reproduce.

According to prophecies in Ezekiel, the Russians will invade Israel with a sizeable force. Ezekiel calls it "a great horde," but this mighty Russian horde will soon turn into a small band of Slavic warriors unless their demographic problems are solved. Regardless of the size of Russia's army,

Ezekiel's prophecy was not incorrect. The invasion will occur, but how strong will Russia be if they wait too much longer?

This same question is plaguing Russian policy makers today. Putin and the Russians want to restore their old empire by expanding the borders, monopolizing energy, and ultimately invading the Middle East—starting with Israel. How could they successfully invade the Middle East without numbers? They must act within the coming decades, if not years.

Putin and the Russian leadership are already trying to solve their demographics dilemma. Their efforts to coerce nearby states into submission, tamper with Ukrainian elections, and invade the nation of Georgia were all attempts to reclaim the Russian power of the Cold War era. Putin knows he has a limited time before his country fades away, which is why a Russian invasion of the Middle East may come quite soon.

Demographics Today

The best-case scenario for the fulfillment of ancient prophecies is the "sooner than later" approach. Europe and the United States, when united, present an opposing force for Westernization and globalization. As geopolitical experts relay, they are nearly invincible when united. Should the Western world wish, it could seek to bring the world closer together tomorrow in global unity.

The longer they dilly-dally, the more Islamic Europe will become, until eventually, it will give way to the eroding cultural force of Islam. If the Tribulation occurs soon after the world wars and the restoration of Israel, as most Bible scholars believe, then Europe must remain Western, and the West must act soon.

Additionally, Russia desperately needs to act sooner rather than later. Most geopolitical experts agree that Russia, although powerful today, is living on borrowed time. Within two decades, Russia will lack the manpower to be an effective nation/state. Putin believes he is mobilizing his nation for continued greatness by their recent exploits, but students of Scripture understand that God himself is setting Russia up to invade the Holy Land. If Europe must act soon, Russia must act much sooner.

Conclusion

THE FUTURE

God's word is the ultimate guide to the future. History has shown that there is no greater prophet, seer, or psychic than the Bible. Biblical prophets have accurately predicted dozens of geopolitical prophecies with one hundred percent accuracy. These predictions will only continue to fulfill themselves in the future. In light of these prophecies, we can see that God's hand has been upon history's path, allowing nations to play out his prophecies with pinpoint accuracy. Nations have also had free will in the matter. Civilizations that have followed God have often prospered, while those who have abandoned him have fallen to their own desires.

Today, both Bible scholars and geopolitical experts reach the same conclusions regarding nations mentioned in the Scriptures. The West, particularly the United States and Western Europe, will eventually seek to implement a global governance system, just as John predicted in Revelation. The nations of Russia, Turkey, and Iran have aligned and will eventually invade Israel and the Middle East, just as Ezekiel predicted. Additionally, the rapidly unfolding geopolitical events, coupled with European demographics, indicates that the return of Christ and the Tribulation are disturbingly near.

God has blessed the Western world mightily over the past 500 years. Western nations such as Great Britain and the United States have been used as evangelists for Christ and protectors of the Jews. Economically, culturally, and militarily, God has allowed the West to thrive. God allowed Great Britain to become a powerful Western leader, only to be replaced by an even greater power, the United States.

America's rise to prominence mirrored the rise of globalization. Today the United States provides the world with stability, both economically and militarily, keeping the forces of chaos at bay. Thanks to the United States, both Israel and Western Europe have been protected, and countless millions have been spared lives of oppression under ruthless dictators elsewhere in the world.

The West, however, has another side—a Mr. Hyde alter ego. Historically, many Western nations have also been enemies of Christ and of Israel. From the Spanish Inquisition to the German holocaust, some Western nations have used their blessings for evil. Once Christ raptures his church from the earth, the darker forces of the Western world will enfold the globe.

Sometime after the world divides into ten districts, the antichrist will come. Using the global system put in place by the Western powers, the antichrist will quickly use the West's superior military to take over large portions of the world. Just as God used Egypt to rescue Jacob and the Hebrews from starvation, only to watch the Egyptians enslave his people centuries later, so too will the Western world turn on the Jews after years of giving them protection.

Current world events also indicate that Russia, Turkey, Iran, and a number of other nations are heading toward a major confrontation with Israel. Fulfilling ancient prophecies, these nations have aligned themselves with one another for the first time in history. Whether or not they realize it, the leaders of these nations are establishing motive, opportunity, and means to invade Israel in the near future.

God could bring Gog and his confederation of nations into the Middle East any number of ways, but the main pursuit of the horde is "plunder." Israel today is full of potential plunder. From newfound oil deposits, to access to the world's holiest places, Israel is a coveted land. Strategically, Israel has always been valued for its centralized location and access to trade routes. Israel sits along the precious waterways of the Mediterranean Sea, the Suez Canal, and the Red Sea—just a stone's throw away from all the oil wealth of the Middle East.

The eternal quest for peace in the Israeli-Palestinian conflict is another magnet for outside powers to conquer Israel. Constantly pressuring, attacking, and undermining Israeli authority, the Palestinians continue to seek outside legitimacy from the UN, the United States, and even Russia. The Palestinians today find allies in Turkey, Iran, and Russia, as they all have strong anti-Jewish passions in their countries, and desire a confrontation with the West.

According to geopolitical strategists, Israel's most implacable enemy—the Arab nations—will not be involved, and many will oppose the invasion. The Arabs lack the military, economic, and political means to attack Israel any time soon. Interdependence with Israel, weak military capability, and the divisive nature of Arab nations highlights that the Arab States will have nothing to do with the invasion. Just as Ezekiel predicted, the merchants of Sheba and Dedan will verbally oppose it.

Only Syria may align itself against the Jews, and that is because of its location near the Golan Heights. Saudi Arabia and the Gulf States will openly oppose the invasion while Egypt and Iraq will maintain a neutral silence. God has bigger plans for both Iraq and Egypt in the future. Moreover, Jordan will play a large role in the Tribulation and will, therefore, be spared from any invasion of Israel.

Additionally, Israel's longtime protector (America) will drop the ball. The very fact that Israel is to be invaded by Russia evidences the quick demise of the Israeli-Western relationship. The United States protects Israel today, but recent trends indicate that this relationship has cooled considerably in the past two years. As Ezekiel predicted, the Western world will not support the invasion but will not protect Israel either.

Perhaps relations will reach such a low point that Israel will be dismissed as a valuable ally in the region. Maybe the Russians will pressure Germany and Eastern Europe to the point that America will even be pressured to sit it out. At the very best, the West is completely surprised by the attack; at the worst, they will ignore their old Jewish friends.

Since their regathering in 1948, Israel has shown that it is more than capable of defending itself. Just as Ezekiel predicted, Israel is living in relative security today. It is more powerful than all of its neighbors, and is strategically sound. The tiny nation's enemies are many, and they are united in satanic opposition to God's ancient people. With assistance from radical Muslims across the globe, as well as the premiere Shiite and Sunni powers, Iran, and Turkey, the Russians will invade the tiny Jewish nation. The Russo-Islamic invasion force will be joined by a great number of nations, including Ethiopia, Sudan, Somalia, Armenia, portions of Eastern Europe and Central Asia, potentially Syria, and an untold number of others. They all will be met with God's destruction.

No one knows exactly when all of this will occur, but Scripture, history, and demographics indicate that it must come soon. The world is declining morally, environmental disasters are on the rise, and Christ's church is wrapping up its seventh and last church age of Laodicea. The past century has seen Jesus's own predictions of world wars and the regathering of Israel come to fulfillment, all of which are impending signs that the end is near.

It is only a matter of time until Western nations seek to unite the world into a global governance system. To combat growing economic crises, world leaders may replace the inept but ideological global unions, known as the UN and the IMF, with a more viable and effective system of world governance. As Revelation indicates, the world quickly splits economically into ten zones or kingdoms. This has been the dream of Western progressives since the early 20th century—a world ruled and administered by the Western, modernized nations of the globe.

The new ten-kingdom earth will be largely controlled by the two most powerful entities in place today, the United States and Western Europe. According to almost unanimous expert opinion, these two forces operating together are unstoppable. Western leaders will spearhead the era of history prophesied by Daniel and John's ten-toed and ten-horned prophecies.

For the Western world to continue governing the world, either through globalization today or ten-administrative kingdoms tomorrow, Europeans need to fix their demographic problems. The prophecies of Scripture indicate that descendants of ancient Rome, not Mohammad, will rule the world of Revelation. The massive arrival of Muslim immigrants into the Western world threatens their very existence. One may conclude that Europeans should move toward their global governance dreams before their nations become too Islamic.

Additionally, in order for Russia to invade Israel in its quest for world domination, it must act before it runs out of soldiers. With one of the lowest birthrates in the world, Russia is on the brink of extinction today. Geopolitical experts point to recent Russian behavior as evidence that Russia is on the move, ready to claim their old sphere of power.

A fulfilled prophecy, when examined by itself, is impressive evidence for God's Word. When nations around the world continue to fulfill ancient predictions, and in a seemingly quick time frame, it presents a strong argument that the strange, bedraggled fellow on the corner may be right. The end may be near. The Rapture—Jesus's promised return for all who have accepted his free gift of salvation and eternal life—may be upon us this week or the next. It may be a few years or a few decades. This will be followed up with the worst seven years of world history. For the Christian believer, Christ's words in Revelation were meant to echo through the ages and down to the end times as a happy reminder: "Look, I am coming soon!" (Revelation 22:7).

WHAT TO DO NEXT?

So what does happen next? If God's plan for history is culminating within our very generation, how should one respond? As Christians, we have the blessed hope of the Rapture—Christ's return for his church before the meltdown of the Tribulation. Christians should also pray for the lost of this world, and for those countries especially in peril, such as Iran, Turkey, and Russia. Again, Russians, evacuate! Hit the beaches of Florida and stay there.

As has been the case throughout most of its history, the nation of Israel is under constant threat of attack. Christians should be praying during these times for both believers and non-believing Jews in that beleaguered nation.

For those who have not yet accepted Christ as savior, I would highly suggest a detailed examination of the facts. The Bible's prophecies have never been proven false. Thousands of years of historical and archeological scrutiny also testify to the Bible's validity. Unlike other religions which require blind faith, God has given us archeological and historical evidence for his claims. In addition, there are the eyewitness accounts of Christ's miracles, including his resurrection from death. Even if the events outlined in this book do not come to fulfillment for another hundred years, it is never too late to accept Christ's free gift of salvation and eternal life.

Christ does not want to condemn humanity to hell (a place reserved initially for fallen angels). Christ came to shed his blood for all of mankind, that they might be restored to the original relationship they were supposed to have with their Creator. By putting their faith in Christ's death on the cross and his resurrection from the grave for salvation rather than their own merits, Christians have a solid escape from the perils of sin. As Romans 3:23 states, "For all have sinned and fall short of the glory of God."

The just, but painful penalty for sin is death and eternal separation from God, as Romans 6:23 states. As any Bible-believing Christian will proclaim, "God so loved the world that he gave his only begotten son, so that whosoever believeth in Him should not perish, but have everlasting life." (John 3:16).

Christ did not make salvation difficult. No amount of work or deeds is necessary. As Ephesians 2:8-9 states, "For it is by grace you have been saved, through faith—and this is not from yourselves, it is the gift of God— not by works, so that no one can boast." The sole work involved in salvation is simply to ask Christ to forgive you of your sins and to become your savior. As Christ puts it, belief and acceptance of his redemption for you results in salvation: "I tell you the truth, whoever hears my word and believes him who sent me has eternal life and will not be condemned; he has crossed over from death to life" (John 5:24).

For those who have found a new faith in Christ Jesus, your best plan of action is to find a good, Bible-believing church to attend and to begin learning what it means to be a devoted disciple of Christ. Give thanks to God, for by becoming a believer in Christ you have had your sins forgiven and will spend eternity with God in heaven. You have also gained an invaluable Lord, friend, and guide throughout this lifetime (and the one after that) in Jesus Christ. Furthermore, you will not endure the trials of the Tribulation, which are to come.

ACKNOWLEDGMENTS

First, to all the folks at Deep River Books, what a tremendous job you have done supporting me in this endeavor. Thank you, Bill Carmichael, for giving me this opportunity. Not only did you get the ball rolling, but you also provided me with a great publishing team and the support necessary to succeed.

I also want to acknowledge Kit Tosello, Lacey Hanes Ogle, and the editing and production team for their extraordinary work making this book a reality. I'm grateful especially to Kit, for keeping me organized and reassuring me, always with an eye on the goal.

A huge thank you to Rhonda Funk and the cover design team for your tremendous job illustrating. What an eye-catching cover design you've created. And I'm grateful to the sales and marketing team for enthusiastically promoting this book and doing a great job of it.

To my editor, Janet Crews, for your patience, dedication, and outstanding editorial talents—thank you. Your abilities were crucial to this book.

Thank you to my childhood pastor and brilliant Bible scholar Dr. J.O. Hosler, for your endorsement, and for instilling in me at a young age the importance of being grounded in sound Biblical doctrine. I would also like to acknowledge Pastor Larry Starkey for your wonderful endorsement and enthusiastic support, and Dr. Arnold Fruchtenbaum, for your invaluable Bible commentaries and sound advice.

I'm overwhelmingly grateful to my family and friends, and to my parents—whose enthusiasm never wanes, and whose support I can always count on. And to a special lady, my wife Ali, who was very patient with me during the writing process.

Last, but not least, I thank my Lord and Savior, Jesus Christ, for giving me the opportunity to serve you through writing and teaching.

NOTES

Introduction

1. "Geopolitics," Merriam-Webster's Dictionary and Thesaurus Online, accessed June 7, 2012, http://www.merriam-webster.com/dictionary/geopolitics, 1.

Chapter 1

1. Arnold G. Fruchtenbaum, *Footsteps of the Messiah; A Study of the Sequence of Prophetic Events. Revised Edition.* (San Antonio: Ariel Ministries Publishing, 2003), 41.

2. Fruchtenbaum, *Footsteps of the Messiah*, 41.

3. John Darwin, *After Tamerlane: The Rise and Fall of Global Empires 1400-2000.* (New York: Bloomsbury Press, 2008), 7.

4. Darwin, *After Tamerlane*, 501.

5. Ibid., 7.

6. Ibid., 480.

Chapter 2

1. George Friedman, *The Next Hundred Years: A Forecast for the 21st Century.* (New York: Double Day Press, 2009), 13.

2. Zbigniew Brzezinski, *The Choice: Global Domination or Global Leadership.* (Cambridge: Basic Books, 2004), 132.

3. George Friedman, *The Next Decade: Where We've Been, and Where We're Going.* (New York: Doubleday Press, 2011), 6.

4. Friedman, *The Next Decade*, 9.

5. Friedman, *The Next Hundred Years*, 18

6. Brzezinski, *The Choice*, 89.

7. Friedman, *The Next Hundred Years*, 18

8. Ibid., 68.

9. Joseph Nyse Jr., *The Future of Power.* (Philadelphia: Perseus Books, 2011), 195.

10. Fruchtenbaum, *Footsteps of the Messiah*, 250.

11. Friedman, *The Next Decade*, 14.

12. Nyse, *The Future of Power,* 56.

13. Ibid., 56.

14. Friedman, *The Next Decade,* 176.

15. Benjamin J. Cohen, *The Geopolitics of Currencies and the Future of the International System.* Paper, Real Institute Conference: Madrid, Spain, 2003, 2.

16. Benjamin J. Cohen, *The Future of Global Currency: The Euro vs. the Dollar.* (New York: Routledge, 2011), 2.

17. Nyse Jr., *The Future of Power,* 58.

18. Friedman, *The Next Decade*, 156.

19. Cohen, *The Geopolitics of Currencies,* 2.

20. Friedman, *Next Hundred Years*, 16.

21. Friedman, *The Next Decade*, 18.

22. Nyse Jr., *The Future of Power*, 192.

23. Ibid., 193.

24. Ibid., 193.

25. Brzezinski, *The Choice,* 149.

26. Ibid., 141.

27. Robert McCrum, *Globish: How English Became the World's Language.* (New York: W.W. Norton and Co, 2010), 11.

28. McCrum, *Globish,* 230.

29. Ibid., 220.

30. Ibid., 209.

31 Ibid., 14.

32. Friedman, *The Next Hundred Years*, 64.

33. Brzezinski, *The Choice,* 183.

34. Ibid., 183.

35. Ibid., 183.

36. Nyse Jr., *The Future of Power,* 97.

37. Friedman, *The Next Decade*, 17.

38. John Phillips, *Exploring the Future: (Commentary Series) A Comprehensive Guide to Bible Prophecy.* (Grand Rapids: Kregel Pub., 2003), 21.

39. Fruchtenbaum, *Footsteps of the Messiah,* 41.

40. Brzezinski, *The Choice,* 189.

41 Julie Duin, "School Prayer Charges Stir Protest." *The Washington Times,* August 14, 2009, accessed August 11, 2011, http://www.washington-times.com/news/2009/aug/14/criminal-prayer-case-stirs-protests/?feat=home_headlines, 1.

42. Pro life foundation, "Abortion Facts and Statistics," last modified November 1, 2007, accessed August 11, 2011, http://prolife.org.ohio-state.edu/Facts.htm.

CHAPTER 3

1. Fruchtenbaum, *Footsteps of the Messiah,* 93.

2 Ibid., 93.

3. Ibid., 93.

4. Joel Rosenberg, *Epicenter: (2.0 Version Updated and Expanded) Why the Current Rumblings in the Middle East Will Change Your Future.* (Carol Stream, IL: Tyndale Pub., 2008), 83.

5. Philips, *Exploring the Future,* 309.

6. Ibid., 310.

7. Ibid., 309.

8. Rosenberg, *Epicenter,* 86.

9. Ibid., 86.

10. Ibid., 86.

11. Philips, *Exploring the Future,* 311.

12. Ibid., 311.

13. Rosenberg, *Epicenter,* 129.

14. Phillips, *Exploring the Future,* 312.

15. Rosenberg, *Epicenter,* 129.

16. Ibid., 129

17. Philips, *Exploring the Future,* 54.

18. George Friedman, "Geopolitics of Israel: Biblical and Modern." *Stratfor,* May 14, 2011, accessed July 10, 2011, http://www.stratfor.com/memberships/115840/analysis/geopolitics_israel_biblical_and_modern.

19. Bret Stephens, "Could Israel become an Energy Giant?" *Wall Street Journal.* April 5, 2011, accessed July 10, 2011, http://online.wsj.com/article/

SB10001424052748703806304576242420737584278.html, 1.

20. Ibid., 1.

21. Phillips, *Exploring the Future,* 314.

22. Friedman, *The Next Decade,* 6.

23. Phillips, *Exploring the Future,* 352.

CHAPTER 4

1. Fruchtenbaum, *Footsteps of the Messiah,* 117.

2. Friedman, "Geopolitics of Israel," 1.

3. Ibid.,1.

4. Ibid.,1.

5. Friedman, *The Next Decade,* 92.

6. Michael Oren, *Faith, Power, and Fantasy: America in the Middle East 1776 to the Present,* (New York: Norton and Co., 2007), 523.

7. Oren, *Faith, Power, and Fantasy,* 526.

CHAPTER 5

1. Rosenberg, *Epicenter,* 95.

2. William F. Engdahl, "The Geopolitical Great Game: Turkey and Russia Moving Closer." *Centre for Research on Globalization,* February 26, 2009, accessed July 10, 2011 http://www.globalresearch.ca/index.php?context=va&aid=12466, 1.

3. Stephen F. Larrabee, "Re-Thinking Russia: Russia, Ukraine, and Central Europe: The Return of Geopolitics." *Columbia School of International Affairs,* Vol. 63, No. 2, (Spring/Summer 2010): 38, accessed July 10, 2011, http://jia.sipa.columbia.edu/russia-ukraine-and-central-europe-return-geopolitics.

4. William F. Engdahl, "Pipeline Geopolitics: The Russia German Nord Stream Strategic Gas Pipeline." *Centre for Research on Globalization,* July 9, 2010, accessed July 10, 2011, http://www.globalresearch.ca/index.php?context=va&aid=20080, 1.

5. Simon Tisdall, "Putin prepares the Russian empire to strike back." *The Guardian,* December 1, 2011, accessed December 3, 2011, http://www.guardian.co.uk/commentisfree/2011/dec/01/putin-prepares-russian-empire?newsfeed=true, 1.

6. Marc Huybrechts, "The Future Face of Geopolitics." *The Brussels Jour-*

nal, 3 (August, 2007): 1, accessed July 10, 2011, http://www.brussel-sjournal.com/node/2284, 1.

7. "Russian soldiers to be woken with 'pleasant music' ahead of elections." *The Telegraph,* December 1, 2011, accessed December 3, 2011, http://www.telegraph.co.uk/news/worldnews/europe/russia/8929796/Russian-soldiers-to-be-woken-with-pleasant-music-ahead-of-elections. html, 1.

8. Ibid., 1.

9. Larabee, "Rethinking Russia," 35.

10. Rosenberg, Epicenter, 102.

11. Ibid., 99.

12. Eli Lake, "Russia Uses Dirty Tricks Despite Reset," *Washington Times,* August 4, 2011, accessed August 6, 2011, http://m.washingtontimes.com/news/2011/aug/4/russia-uses-dirty-tricks-despite-us-reset/.

13. Ibid., 1.

14. Larabee, "Rethinking Russia," 36.

15. Global Trends conference, "Global Trends 2025: The National Intelligence Council's 2025 Project." *National Intelligence Council,* (November 2008): 39, Washington DC: US Government Printing Office, accessed July 13, 2011, http://www.dni.gov/nic/NIC_2025_project.html.

16. Mark Steyn, *America Alone: The End of the World as We Know it.* (Washington DC: Regnery Publishing, 2009), ix.

17. Friedman, *The Next Hundred Years,* 117.

18. Steyn, *America Alone,* 27.

19. Larrabee, "Rethinking Russia," 38.

20. Ibid., 38.

21. Friedman, *The Next Decade,* 122.

22. Tisdall, "Putin prepares the Russian Empire to strike back," 1

23. Andrej Kreutz, "The Geopolitics of Post-Soviet Russia and the Middle East." *Arab Studies Quarterly,* (Winter, 2002): 1, accessed July 10, 2011, http://findarticles.com/p/articles/mi_m2501/is_1_24/ai_93458168/, 1.

24. Kreutz, "Geopolitics of post-Soviet Russia and the Middle East," 1.

25. Ibid., 1.

26. Engdahl, "Geopolitical Great Game," 1.

27. George Friedman, "Shifting Geopolitics: The Rise of Russia and

Turkey." *Stratfor,* March 18, 2009, accessed July 10, 2011, http://www.marketoracle.co.uk/Article9509.html, 1.

28. Marc Herzog, "FPC Briefing: From Foe to Friend- the Volte Face in Turkish-Russian Relations over the last Decade." *Foreign Policy Centre,* accessed July 13, 2011, http://fpc.org.uk/articles/468, 1.

29. Rosenberg, *Epicenter,* 135.

30. Ibid., 106.

31. Ibid., xx.

32. "Russian anti-terror Troops reportedly enter Syria." *Fox News,* March 19. 2012, accessed March 20, 2012, http://www.foxnews.com/world/2012/03/19/russian-troops-reportedly-enter-syria/, 1.

33. Reza Akhlaghi, "Iran: Geopolitical Conundrum." *Global Brief,* December 8, 2009, accessed July 10, 2011, http://globalbrief.ca/blog/2009/12/08/iran-geopolitical-conundrum/, 1.

34. Rosenberg, *Epicenter,* 148.

CHAPTER 6

1. Bernard Lewis, *Jews of Islam,* (Princeton: Princeton University Press, 1987), 136.

2. Friedman, "Shifting Geopolitics," 1.

3. Ibid., 1.

4. Akhlaghi, "Iran: Geopolitical Conundrum," 1.

5. Friedman, *The Next Decade,* 117.

6. Soner Cagaptay, "Is Turkey Leaving the West? An Islamist Foreign Policy Puts Ankara at Odds With its Former Allies." *Council on Foreign Affairs,* (26 October 2009): 1, accessed July 13, 2011, http://www.foreignaffairs.com/articles/65661/soner-cagaptay/is-turkey-leaving-the-west.

7. Herzog, "From Foe to Friend," 3.

8. Chris Mitchell, "Turkey Election Sparks Fears of Islamic Caliphate." *CBN News,* 11 June 2011, accessed July 13, 2011, http://www.cbn.com/cbnnews/insideisrael/2011/June/Turkey-Election-Sparks-Fears-of-Islamic-Caliphate-/.

9. Ibid., 1.

10. Cagaptay, "Is Turkey Leaving the West?" 1.

11. Ibid., 1.

12. Johan Spanner, "Turkey," *New York Times,* December 3, 2011, accessed December 3, 2011, http://topics.nytimes.com/top/news/international/countriesandterritories/turkey/index.html, 1.

13. Anat Lapidot-Firilla, "Sinking Turkey-Israel Relations." *Jerusalem Post,* July 6, 2010, accessed July 13, 2011, http://www.jpost.com/Opinion/Op-EdContributors/Article.aspx?id=177087.

14. George Friedman, "Turkey's Election and Strained US Relations." *Stratfor,* June 14, 2011, accessed July 10, 2011, http://www.stratfor.com/weekly/20110613-turkeys-elections-and-strained-us-relations.

15. Cagaptay, "Is Turkey leaving the West?" 1.

16. "Persecution in Turkey," *The Voice of the Martyrs,* accessed August 11, 2011, http://www.persecution.net/turkey.htm.

17. Daniel Blake, "Turkey Christian Missionaries Horrifically Tortured Before Killed." *Christian Today,* April 26, 2007, accessed August 11, 2011, http://www.christiantoday.com/article/turkey.christian.missionaries.horrifically.tortured.before.killings/10523.htm.

18. Harold Rhode, "Turkey: Erdogan's New "Ottoman Region,"" *Hudson New York,* July 13, 2011, accessed August 11, 2011, http://www.hudson-ny.org/2259/turkey-erdogan-ottoman-region.

19. Oren Dorell, "'Honor Killings' in USA Raise Concerns," *USA Today,* November 30, 2009, accessed August 11, 2011, http://www.usatoday.com/news/nation/2009-11-29-honor-killings-in-the-US_N.htm.

Chapter 7

1. Bernard Lewis, *From Babel to Dragomans: Interpreting the Middle East.* (New York: Oxford University Press, 2004), 46.

2. Lewis, *From Babel to Dragomans,* 44.

3. Ibid., 156.

4. Ibid., 228.

5. Robert Baer, *The Devil We Know; Dealing with the New Iranian Superpower.* (New York: Crown Publishers, 2009), 54.

6. Friedman, *The Next Decade,* 82.

7. Ibid., 68.

8. Ibid., 110.

9. Rosenberg, *Epicenter,* 121.

10. Friedman, *The Next Decade*, 66.

11. Ibid., 111.

12. Ibid., 111.

13. Baer, *The Devil We Know*, 148.

14. Ibid., 142.

15. Ibid., 55.

16. Ibid., 175.

17. Robin Wright, *Dreams and Shadows: The Future of the Middle East.* (New York: Penguin Press, 2008), 52.

CHAPTER 8

1"Global Christianity – A Report on the Size and Distribution of the World's Christian Population," *The Pew Forum on Religion and Public Life,* December 19, 2011, accessed June 25, 2012, http://www.pewforum.org/Christian/Global-Christianity-preface.aspx, 1.

2. Friedman, *The Next Decade*, 218.

3. Ibid., 220.

4. Ariel Cohen, "Russia's New Scramble for Africa." *Wall Street Journal,* July 22009, accessed July 13, 2011, http://online.wsj.com/article/SB124639219666775441.html, 1.

5. Ibid.,1.

6. US State Department, International Religious Freedom Report, Bureau of Democracy, Human Rights, and Labor, (2004): 1, accessed August 13, 2011, http://www.state.gov/g/drl/rls/irf/2004/35355.htm.

7. Michael Cook, "Will Ethiopia Become a Majority Muslim Nation? *Mercator.net,* December 7 2009, accessed August 13, 2011, http://www.mercatornet.com/demography/view/6190/, 1.

CHAPTER 9

1. Bzrezinski, *The Choice,* 89.

2. Ibid., 220.

3. Larrabee, "Rethinking Russia," 47.

4. Friedman, *The Next Decade*, 134.

5.   James Sperling, "Germany and America in the 21st Century; Repeating the Post-War Patterns of Conflict and Cooperation," *German Politics,* Vol. 19, No. 1, (March 2010): 56, accessed August 13, 2011, http://www.tandfonline.com/doi/abs/10.1080/09644001003588598#preview, 1.

CHAPTER 10

1.   Tarek Osman, *Egypt on the Brink: From Nasser to Mubarak.* (London: Yale University Press, 2011), 82.

2.   Osman, *Egypt on the Brink,* 83.

3.   Ibid., 86.

4.   Wright, *Dreams and Shadows*, 98.

5.   Osman, *Egypt on the Brink*, 80.

6.   Ibid., 112.

7.   Friedman, *The Next Decade*, 99.

8.   Wright, *Dreams and Shadows*, 241.

9.   Ibid., 240.

10. Ibid., 244.

11. Ibid., 244.

12. Friedman, *The Next Decade,* 88.

13. "Israeli-Palestinian Conflict," *ProCon.org,* September 9, 2010, accessed August 13, 2011, http://israelipalestinian.procon.org/view.resource.php?resourceID=000636, 1.

14. Fruchtenbaum, *Footsteps of the Messiah*, 290.

15. Ibid., 291.

16. Ibid., 292.

CHAPTER 11

1.   Fruchtenbaum, *Footsteps of the Messiah*, 234.

2.   Ibid., 234.

3.   Ibid., 234.

4.   Rosenberg, *Epicenter,* 174.

5.   Ibid.,180.

6.   Ibid., 174.

7.   Dave Itzhoff, "Project Created to Restore Ancient Babylon." *New York Times*, January 7, 2009, accessed August 13, 2011, http://artsbeat.blogs.

nytimes.com/2009/01/07/project-created-to-restore-ancient-babylon/, 1.

8. Robert F. Ebel, "Geopolitics and Energy in Iraq." *Center for Strategic and International Studies,* 5 (August 2010): 1, accessed July 10, 2011, http://csis.org/publication/geopolitics-and-energy-iraq, 1.

9. Ebel, "Geopolitics and Energy in Iraq," 1.

10. Ibid., 1.

CHAPTER 12

1. Fruchtenbaum, *Footsteps of the Messiah,* 240.

2. Friedman, *The Next Decade*, 174.

3. Ibid., 176.

4. Ibid., 176.

5. Friedman, *The Next Hundred Years*, 96.

6. Friedman, *The Next Decade*, 174.

7. Ibid., 174.

8. Brzezinski, *The Choice*, 110.

9. Ibid., 113.

10. Nyse Jr., *The Future of Power*, 165.

CHAPTER 13

1. Steyn, *America Alone*, 2.

2. Ibid., ix.

3. Ibid., 34.

4. Ibid., 76.

5. Ibid., xv.

6. "Global Trends 2025," 45.

7. Steyn, *America Alone,* 2.

SELECTED BIBLIOGRAPHY

Aklaghi, Reza. "Iran: Geopolitical Conundrum." Global Brief, 8 December 2009, http://globalbrief.ca/blog/2009/12/08/iran-geopolitical-conundrum/ (Accessed July 10, 2011).

Baer, Robert. The Devil We Know; Dealing with the New Iranian Superpower. New York: Crown Publishers, 2009.

Blake, Daniel, "Turkey Christian Missionaries Horrifically Tortured Before Killed." Christian Today, 26 April, 2007. http://www.christiantoday.com/article/turkey.christian.missionaries.horrifically.tortured.before.killings/10 523.htm, (Accessed August 11, 2011).

Brzezinski, Zbigniew. The Choice: Global Domination or Global Leadership. Cambridge: Basic Books, 2004.

Cagaptay, Soner. "Is Turkey Leaving the West? An Islamist Foreign Policy Puts Ankara at Odds With its Former Allies." Council on Foreign Affairs, 26 October (2009), http://www.foreignaffairs.com/articles/65661/soner-cagaptay/is-turkey-leaving-the-west (Accessed July 13, 2011).

Cohen, Ariel. "Russia's New Scramble for Africa." Wall Street Journal, 2 July 2009, http://online.wsj.com/article/SB124639219666775441.html (Accessed July 13, 2011).

Cohen, Benjamin J. The Future of Global Currency: The Euro vs. the Dollar. New York: Routledge, 2011.

————. The Geopolitics of Currencies and the Future of the International System. Paper, Real Institute Conference: Madrid, Spain, 2003.

Cook, Michael. "Will Ethiopia become a Majority Muslim Nation? Mercator.net, 7

December 2009. http://www.mercatornet.com/demography/view/6190/ (Accessed August 13, 2011).

Cordesman, Anthony. "The Uncertain Security Situation in Iraq: Trends in Violence, Casualties, and Iraqi Perceptions." *Center for Strategic and International Studies* 17 February 2010, http://csis.org/publication/uncertain-security-situation-iraq (Accessed July 13, 2011).

Darwin, John. *After Tamerlane: The Rise and Fall of Global Empires 1400-2000*. New York: Bloomsbury Press, 2008.

Dorell, Oren, "'Honor Killings' in USA Raise Concerns," *USA Today,* 30 November 2009, http://www.usatoday.com/news/nation/2009-11-29-honor-killings-in-the-US_N.htm (Accessed August, 11, 2011).

Duin, Julie. "School Prayer Charges Stir Protest." *The Washington Times,* 14, August, 2009. http://www.washingtontimes.com/news/2009/aug/14/criminal-prayer-case-stirs-protests/?feat=home_headlines (Accessed, August 11, 2011).

Ebel, Robert E. "Geopolitics and Energy in Iraq." *Center for Strategic and International Studies,* 5 August 2010, http://csis.org/publication/geopolitics-and-energy-iraq (Accessed July 10, 2011).

Engdahl, William F. "Pipeline Geopolitics: The Russia German Nord Stream Strategic Gas Pipeline." *Centre for Research on Globalization,* 9 July 2010, http://www.globalresearch.ca/index.php?context=va&aid=20080 (Accessed July 10, 2011).

———. "The Geopolitical Great Game: Turkey and Russia Moving Closer." *Centre for Research on Globalization,* 26 February 2009, http://www.globalresearch.ca/index.php?context=va&aid=12466 (Accessed July 10, 2011).

Fox News, "Russian anti-terror Troops reportedly enter Syria." *Fox News,* March 19, 2012, http://www.foxnews.com/world/2012/03/19/russian-troops-reportedly-enter-syria/. (accessed March 20, 2012)

Friedman, George. *The Next Decade: Where We've Been, and Where We're Going.* New York: Doubleday Press, 2011.

———. *The Next Hundred Years: A forecast for the 21st Century.* New York: Double Day Press, 2009.

———. "Shifting Geopolitics: The Rise of Russia and Turkey." *Stratfor,* 18 March 2009, http://www.marketoracle.co.uk/Article9509.html (Accessed July 10, 2011).

———. "Turkey's Election and Strained US Relations." *Stratfor,* 14 June 2011, http://www.stratfor.com/weekly/20110613-turkeys-elections-and-strained-us-relations (Accessed July 10, 2011).

———. "Geopolitics of Israel: Biblical and Modern." *Stratfor,* 14 May 2011, http://www.stratfor.com/memberships/115840/ analysis/geopolitics_israel_biblical_and_modern (Accessed July 10, 2011).

Friedman, Thomas. *The World Is Flat: (Updated and Expanded) A Brief History of the 21st Century.* New York: Farrar, Straus, and Giroux, 2006.

Fruchtenbaum, Arnold G. *Footsteps of the Messiah; A Study of the Sequence of Prophetic Events. Revised Edition.* San Antonio: Ariel Ministries Publishing, 2003.

"Global Trends 2025: The National Intelligence Council's 2025 Project." *National Intelligence Council,* November 2008, Washington DC: US Government Printing Office, http://www.dni.gov/nic/NIC_2025_project.html (Accessed July 13, 2011).

Herzog, Marc. "FPC Briefing: From Foe to Friend- the Volte Face in Turkish-Russian Relations over the last Decade." *Foreign Policy Centre,* date unknown http://fpc.org.uk/articles/468 (Accessed July 13, 2011).

Huybrechts, Marc. "The Future Face of Geopolitics." *The Brussels Journal,* 3 August, 2007, http://www.brusselsjournal.com/node/2284 (Accessed July 10, 2011).

"Israeli-Palestinian Conflict," ProCon.org, 9 September, 2010, http://israeli-palestinian.procon.org/view.resource.php?resourceID=000636 (Accessed August 13, 2011).

Itzhoff, Dave "Project Created to Restore Ancient Babylon." *New York Times*, 7 January 2009, http://artsbeat.blogs.nytimes.com/2009/ 01/07/project-created-to-restore-ancient-babylon/, (Accessed August 13, 2011).

King, Ian. "Oil Shale Reserves can turn Israel into a Major World Producer." *The Australian,* 21 March, 2011, http://www.theaustralian.com.au/business-old/mining-energy/oil-shale-reserves-can-turn-israel-into-major-world-producer/story-e6frg9ef-1226025327281 (Accessed July 10, 2011).

Kreutz, Andrej. "The Geopolitics of Post-Soviet Russia and the Middle East." *Arab Studies Quarterly,* (Winter, 2002). http://findarticles.com/p/articles/mi_m2501/is_1_24/ai_93458168/ (Accessed July 10, 2011).

Lake, Eli. "Russia Uses Dirty Tricks Despite Reset," *Washington Times,* 4 August, 2011, http://m.washingtontimes.com/news/2011/aug/4/russia-uses-dirty-tricks-despite-us-reset/, (accessed August 6, 2011).

Lapidot-Firilla, Anat. "Sinking Turkey-Israel Relations." *Jerusalem Post,* 6 July, 2010 http://www.jpost.com/Opinion/Op-EdContributors/Article.aspx?id=177087 (Accessed July 13, 2011).

Larrabee, Stephen F. "Re-Thinking Russia: Russia, Ukraine, and Central Europe: The Return of Geopolitics." *Columbia School of International Affairs,* Vol. 63, No. 2, (Spring/Summer 2010): pgs 33-52. http://jia.sipa.columbia.edu/russia-ukraine-and-central-europe-return-geopolitics (Accessed July 10, 2011).

Lewis, Bernard. *From Babel to Dragomans: Interpreting the Middle East.* New York: Oxford University Press, 2004.

———. *The Jews of Islam.* Princeton: Princeton University Press, 1987.

McCrum, Robert. *Globish: How English Became the World's Language.* New York: W.W. Norton and Co., 2010

Bibliography

Miriam-Webster Dictionary and Thesaurus Online, http://www.merriam-webster.com/(Accessed June 7, 2012).

Mitchell, Chris. "Turkey Election Sparks Fears of Islamic Caliphate." *CBN News*, 11 June 2011, http://www.cbn.com/cbnnews/insideisrael/2011/June/Turkey-Election-Sparks-Fears-of-Islamic-Caliphate-/ (Accessed July 13, 2011).

Nyse, Joseph Jr. *The Future of Power.* Philadelphia: Perseus Books, 2011.

Oren, Michael. *Faith, Power, and Fantasy: America in the Middle East 1776 to the Present.* New York: Norton and Co., 2007.

Osman, Tarek. *Egypt on the Brink: From Nasser to Mubarak.* London: Yale University Press, 2011.

"Persecution in Turkey," The Voice of the Martyrs, http://www.persecution.net/turkey.htm, (Accessed, August 11, 2011).

Phillips, John. *Exploring the Future: (Commentary Series) A Comprehensive Guide to Bible Prophecy.* Grand Rapids: Kregel Pub., 2003.

The Pro Life Foundation, "Abortion Facts and Statistics," 1 November, 2007. http://prolife.org.ohio-state.edu/Facts.htm (Accessed August 11, 2011), 1.

Rhode, Harold, "Turkey: Erdogan's New "Ottoman Region,"" *Hudson New York,* 13 July 2011, http://www.hudson-ny.org/2259/turkey-erdogan-ottoman-region, (Accessed August 11, 2011).

Rosenberg, Joel C. *Epicenter: (2.0 Version Updated and Expanded) Why the Current Rumblings in the Middle East Will Change Your Future.* Carol Stream, IL: Tyndale Pub., 2008.

Spanner, Johan. "Turkey," *New York Times,* December 3, 2011, http://topics.nytimes.com/top/news/international/countriesandterritories/turkey/index.html (Accessed December 3, 2011).

Stephens, Bret. "Could Israel become an Energy Giant?" *Wall Street Journal.*

5 April 2011, http://online.wsj.com/article/SB1000142405274870380
63045762424207375584278.html (Accessed July 10, 2011).

Sperling, James. "Germany and America in the 21st Century; Repeating the Post-War Patterns of Conflict and Cooperation," *German Politics,* Vol. 19, No. 1, (March 2010): pgs 53-71. http://www.tandfonline.com/doi/abs/ 10.1080/09644001003588598#preview (Accessed August 13, 2011).

Steyn, Mark. *America Alone: The End of the World as We Know it.* Washington DC: Regnery Publishing, 2009.

The Telegraph. "Russian Soldiers to be woken with 'pleasant music' ahead of elections." *The Telegraph,* December 1, 2011, http://www.telegraph.co.uk/ news/worldnews/europe/russia/8929796/Russian-soldiers-to-be-woken-with-pleasant-music-ahead-of-elections.html (Accessed December 3, 2011).

Tisdall, Simon. "Putin prepares the Russian empire to strike back." *The Guardian,* December 1, 2011, http://www.guardian.co.uk/commentisfree/ 2011/dec/01/putin-prepares-russian-empire?newsfeed=true (Accessed December 3, 2011).

US State Department, International Religious Freedom Report, Bureau of Democracy, Human Rights, and Labor, 2004 http://www.state.gov/g/drl/ rls/irf/2004/35355.htm (Accessed August 13, 2011).

Wright, Robin. *Dreams and Shadows: The Future of the Middle East.* New York: Penguin Press, 2008.

Ziyad, Abu Amr. *Islamic Fundamentalism in the West Bank and Gaza: Muslim Brotherhood and Islamic Jihad (Indiana Series in Arab and Islamic Studies).* Bloomington: Indiana University Press, 1994.